MW00712516

UNDERSTANDING THE ASIAN MANAGER

Working with the movers of the Pacific century

HARI BEDI

To
Donna,
Best wishes.
y the author
HBedi
Sept. 24, 1991

ALLEN & UNWIN

To my daughter, Anjali

© Hari Bedi, 1991
This book is copyright under the Berne Convention. No reproduction without permission.

First published in 1991
Allen & Unwin Pty Ltd
8 Napier Street, North Sydney, NSW 2059 Australia

National Library of Australia
Cataloguing-in-Publication entry:

Bedi, Hari.
  Understanding the Asian manager.

  Includes index.
  ISBN 1 86373 029 X.

  1. Executives—Asia. 2. Management—Asia. I. Title.

658.409095

Set in 10/11 pt Garamond by Graphicraft Typesetters Ltd., Hong Kong
Printed by Dah Hua Co. Ltd., in Hong Kong

Contents

Preface

This book is largely based on my personal experiences of managing in a multinational corporate environment. I have been privileged to work with associates of several different nationalities. Many of them were outstanding managers. A relatively small number, however, were incredibly insensitive and ethnocentric. They were totally inept in handling human relations in a multicultural setting. Both types appear in this book. They are real life people, even though their names—such as Pickle, Uncle Tim, Jaye Shagun, and Jambon—have been changed to avoid any possible embarrassment. In the main though, most people are described by their real names and designations.

My interviews with over 50 senior Asian managers and chief executives are the second most important source. I was greatly struck during these interviews by the strong endorsement of my own feelings and views. It was gratifying to know that I was not pursuing a narrow and personal theme. A deeper understanding of the cultural context in which multinational managers operate was widely held as one of the most important and broad-based issues facing the world of business and commerce. The very fact that people of such stature as Paron Israsena, president of Siam Cement; Anat Arbhabhirama, governor of the Petroleum Authority of Thailand; Chin Teck Huat, CEO of Intraco in Singapore; Alan Yeo, chairman of Yeo Hiap Seng; V. Krishnamurthy, chairman of the Steel Authority of India; Tan Sri Hamzah Sendut, director of ICI group of companies in Malaysia; Rizalino Navarro, chairman of SGV & Co; and Corazon de la Paz; senior partner of Price Waterhouse in the Philippines, freely gave their time and advice is proof of the importance they attach to this subject.

It will take too much space to mention them all here; their valuable contribution speaks for itself in various chapters. Their remarks quoted here were made during my interviews with them, though to avoid repetition I have not specifically stated it in each case. For example, the observations made by Gaston Ortigas, former Dean of the Asian Institute of Management, were made by him during our lengthy and most enjoyable conversation, and not lifted from a text book. When I do use a brief extract from some book, I have clearly identified both the book and the author. I must point out, however, that such references are only in passing and are not used as basic material. *Understanding the Asian Manager* makes no claim to be a work of academic research.

I am particularly grateful to two men in two different ways. One is Michael O'Neill, editor-in-chief of *Asiaweek*. I first approached him four years ago to discuss the idea of this book. He was very enthusiastic, but suggested that I should start by writing a weekly column for the magazine. The discipline of preparing a column week after week for three years proved indispensable when I finally sat down to complete the manuscript. The other person is Jim Walker, my friend and former boss. Jim retired a few years ago as the president of Exxon Chemical Asia Pacific. He taught me one of the core messages of this book: one cannot be a good manager without being a good human being.

Most of all I am thankful to my wife and two children who have shared with me a thousand joys and frustrations of growing into an 'international' family. I have been especially influenced by my daughter who believes that people, no matter how high their accomplishments, are a failure if they are poor in human relations. In dedicating this book to her, I am hopeful of the next generation's prospects of becoming truly multicultural.

1 The multicultural minefield

Most multinational companies have for long held the view that a person who is proficient in certain techniques and skills can be an effective manager anywhere in the world. Of late, however, there has been a growing awareness that to be successful, managers must adapt their expertise to the cultural and economic context in which they operate. References to national or regional variations, such as the American or European style of management, have become common. Along with economic development, Asia is also evolving its own style of management. A blend of old and new, it has strong elements of Asian cultures and values.

To succeed in Asia, multinational managers must have some understanding of the special features of this approach. Too often their only guide is stereotyped advice from 'instant' experts on Asia. Such counselling dwells on surface matters such as warnings against patting a Japanese on the back, turning the sole of one's shoe towards a Malay, or touching the head of a Thai. The prerequisite for business success today, however, is a far deeper understanding of cultural differences.

Yet we face a paradox: despite all the talk about global village and internationalisation of labour and capital, behaviour patterns everywhere are still largely determined by local cultures. Multinational managers who may work with colleagues of ten different nationalities in building a business for the twenty-first century have to understand traits that have their origin in the nineteenth century and often in the still more distant past.

Dealing with people who have a social and cultural background similar to ours is difficult enough. The problem is vastly magnified when one is operating in a multicultural environment. Preconceived notions which managers may have carried securely in their minds since childhood can make the corporate arena more explosive than a minefield. What they most need to learn is often precisely what they think they already know.

The primary sources of Western images of Asia have historically

1

been Westerners. Some of these images have not moved much beyond the China of the days of Marco Polo and the India of the Raj. In his book *Western Images of China*, Colin Mackerras says that 'the rapid technological progress which resulted from the Industrial Revolution made most Westerners extremely sure of themselves and led them to look down on those they regarded as backward or inferior, which included the Chinese. 'Western attitudes were entirely consistent with the imperialism of the day', he adds. 'Orientalism' (viewing Asia from an ethnocentric Western perspective) is still very much in vogue.

It is simple to continue to live with old perceptions. Cultural understanding is difficult and sometimes painful to attain, but the rewards can be also high. Raymonde Carroll points out in her book *Cultural Misunderstandings* that 'one of the great advantages of cultural analysis, aside from that of expanding our horizons, is that of transforming our cultural misunderstandings from a source of occasionally deep wounds into a fascinating and inexhaustible exploration of the other.'

Sometime ago I met a group of American managers visiting Asia on a fact-finding mission. One of them was the vice president of employee relations. He kept on quizzing me about frictions between Asian employees of different nationalities. I had to explain patiently that no doubt there are differences but that these managers work together quite effectively in international companies. They all speak English and have had the benefit of training and experience in modern management. More importantly, they share a great many common values. Surface differences often mask deep similarities. Most Asians share a sense of history. They believe in mutual obligations and have strong feelings of moral debt. They instinctively avoid conflict of loyalties as it causes them great emotional distress. They deeply admire the quality of spiritual fortitude. Nevertheless, the old stereotype perceptions, fanned by pseudo-academic research, continue to persist. The visitors had just read a copy of one such study prepared by an international business organisation. It contained every trite and shopworn prejudice. They mentioned the study over a lunch attended by seven or eight Asian managers of different nationalities, all of whom were unanimous in their condemnation of the perpetuation of those old perceptions.

Multinational managers must delve deeper into Asian values. Asian societies are essentially traditional and differ dramatically from pragmatic societies, such as the USA, which are technologically oriented. Asian societies place an emphasis on group participation rather than individual achievement. They are guided by old customs and beliefs. Tradition provides an underpinning to almost everything that is considered important in life. Religion, history, ancient beliefs, language, and the family provide an enduring cultural framework.

Globalisation and conformity

Asian managers do not want the wave of globalisation to become another form of colonialism. Everybody today wants to go global and Asia is seen as the great untapped opportunity. Many foreigners believe Asians will buy any product or use any service that is annointed with a touch of Western know-how, or is identified with America or Europe. They dream not of a local production or partnership, but of a vast centrally-controlled market. The Asian connection, if it is sought at all, is seen as being of secondary importance. The notion is that you don't have to adapt your products since Asians will only too willingly change their habits.

In the last 25 years, multinationals operating in Asia have changed very little in comparison with the external environment in which they do business. Economic progress and political stability have provided greater pride and confidence to many countries in the region. Foreign companies no longer enjoy the exclusive technological edge they once had. Special privileges for manufacturing investments are becoming hard to justify. Marketing is much more complex than simply using a string of local distributors. Foreign companies have to provide a high degree of leadership and motivation to Asian managers to gain their participation and commitment to succeed in the future. But the essentially subservient status of local managers remains unchanged.

A global business cannot simply have its headquarters in one country and treat the rest of the world as one big market. Local autonomy is fast becoming the key to successful globalisation. The traditional pyramid, with its headquarters at the apex and its branch offices below, is destined to become a thing of the past. The existing management rules were built on the Western cultural heritage. Using English as the international business language bestows a built-in advantage upon many multinational managers. Therefore it is easy for them to fall into the trap of thinking they represent universality and expect everyone else to conform. But the global corporate chest of the future must beat with many hearts, or it will die.

Meanwhile, managers working in a multicultural environment in Asia can make both themselves and others happier at work by being sensitive and aware of basic differences in the attitudes and behaviour patterns of their colleagues. Cognitive psychologists emphasise that intelligence comes in multiple forms: interpersonal (understanding others), intrapersonal (understanding oneself), physical (working with one's hands), verbal and logical–mathematical. But it is still not widely stressed that different cultures admire and respond to different forms of intelligence. In Asia interpersonal skills are valued most and a manager who fails to grasp this simple truth is either headed towards personal disaster or is destined to make a lot of people very unhappy.

In *One-on-one with Andy Grove*, the head of Intel advises the reader to look for another job if the boss lays down the law then proceeds to break it, or if he or she is possessed of an evil temper. He also suggests that if something is annoying you, you should confront the offender with your problem and talk it over. Such advice does not travel across cultural borders. Neither changing a job nor confonting the boss is undertaken lightly in Asia. Most Asians keep the hurt within themselves. They expect the boss to know how they feel. They are culturally conditioned to be humble. Often incalculable damage is done before inexperienced multinational managers realise their mistakes. As a manager you cannot avoid dealing with people. But with a little effort you can convert a potentially frustrating activity into a most rewarding one.

2 The corporate and cultural framework

It was Jaye Shagun's twenty-fifth anniversary with Westbig Corporation, one of the world's largest multinationals. As he sat in the
company's Asia-Pacific regional office, he glanced at the nuclear-
powered American carrier anchored in Hong Kong harbour. It
looked incongruous in the midst of sampans, junks, and Chinese
sailboats which had remained unchanged for centuries. So many
things in Hong Kong, he thought, brought the contrast between old
and new into sharp focus. On this day, a milestone in his career, Jaye
had reason to reflect on some contrasts in his own life. He could not
help thinking about the twists and turns that had shaped the long
journey.

He had started his career with the company after completing an
engineering degree from the USA. During the 25 years, he had been
assigned to several places in Asia, finally ending up in the regional
head office. There was so much to remember about the people and
events that had moulded his attitudes. He recalled with a wry smile
his very first month with the company when he nearly lost his job
simply through trying to be polite. Interviewed and hired at the company's head office, he had worked there for a few weeks before
returning home. One evening, while having a drink at a hotel near the
office, he saw two expatriate managers of the company arriving at the
bar. He greeted them warmly and offered to buy drinks. They looked
surprised but joined him all the same. The conversation was stilted
and Jaye felt most uncomfortable. Back at the office next morning he
found out it was not the custom for expatriate senior managers to mix
socially with their subordinates. Moreover, the hotel bar was a ren-
dezvous for foreigners and it was unusual to see young local people
there. The incident set a pattern for the relationship between Jaye and
his expatriate managers in the early part of his career. As the years
went by, socio-economic conditions improved and his own position
as head of department greatly changed the relationship. And yet only
a few days previously Jaye had found himself advising a younger
colleague to be careful in his relations with expatriate managers. He

had felt it important to explain that the relationship between a senior Asian manager and his subordinates is conditioned more by culture and custom than by organisational structure or corporate practice. But the relationship between Asians and expatriate managers was pretty much always part of the organisational equation.

Over the years Jaye had worked with hundreds of managers of different nationalities. He had often wondered why it was so difficult for expatriates to accept that Asian employees are culturally different. How many times had Jaye heard a senior expatriate remark that this or that Asian manager was status conscious, or tended to be overly sensitive, or had reverted to their own brand of logic? Performance evaluations based on such perceptions were always seen by Asian managers as ignorance.

He wondered why so few foreigners take the trouble to establish a personal equation at the outset to help build the mutual trust so valued in Asia. Ideally, each must learn from the other. European or American managers must accept that it will take them a very long time to understand the insular Asian cultures. How tiresome are the 'experts' who, after a year or two, know everything because they have downed *maotais* at a Beijing banquet or eaten chilli crabs in Malaysia with their fingers! Most successful managers display humility about their lack of knowledge. They rely on their Asian associates for orientation.

Jaye's reminiscences on his twenty-fifth anniversary with the company are not very different from the way most Asian managers working in a multinational environment feel every day. Whether they are Chinese, Filipinos, Indians, Indonesians, Japanese, Koreans, Malays, or Thais, these managers share a common corporate and cultural framework.

Corporate hurdles

The first problem Asian managers face is the tendency on the part of expatriate managers just assigned to Asia to 'retreat to the familiar'— to recreate the past. Bill Wilson, recognised by his company as a top marketer of personal computers in England, is transferred to Asia as a regional manager. He immediately sets out to repeat his success by falling back on the methods that had proved effective in his previous job. He is conditioned by his prior business experience and feels secure in following a familiar path. His aim is to bring everything closer to that with which he is accustomed.

The second hurdle is to do with economics: differences in salaries and perks. When employees are classified as expatriates, locals, and third country nationals, it acts against all good intentions to develop a truly multinational team.

A third problem concerns corporate culture. Understanding other cultures is made difficult in an international company because of the pursuit of a common business aim and an overlay of company values and behaviour. The dominant factor in that behaviour is the culture of the home office of the organisation. Multinationals have done much to develop professional management, but senior positions in most companies are still held by managers who belong to the home cultures of these companies. The Japanese occupy all the top positions in Japanese companies. Americans are at the top of American multinationals. The subsidiaries of British multinationals are managed largely by Brits.

Fourthly is the fact that the business approach of most multinationals is dominated by their home office. Major decisions are made at the head office by senior executives, most of whom have never worked abroad. Their emphasis may be on short-term gain versus long-term profit, and smaller and secure business segments versus the larger market share. Their perception of political and economic risks in various countries is usually at variance with the views of the management of their overseas subsidiaries.

Individual managers can help influence their companies to bridge these barriers. Even within these constraints they can be quite effective if they have an understanding of the basic differences shaped by cultural factors.

Cultural constraints

Asia is the birthplace of some of the world's great religions. There, they remain the golden yardstick by which all human behaviour, including conduct in the business world, is judged. 'Instant' experts advise that it is dangerous for expatriates to talk about religion to Asians as they may run the risk of offending others. On the contrary, expatriates would go up in their Asian colleagues' esteem if they show an interest in learning about their religions.

History, including the collective memory of the experiences of colonialism (defeat in the case of the Japanese), has shaped many contemporary Asian attitudes. An Asian manager's reaction is often rooted in the past. The colonial era is blamed for having imposed Western values on Asian societies. Most of these countries still have special names for foreigners which unfortunately are not always flattering: *gweilo* in Hong Kong, *geijin* in Japan, *farang* in Thailand, *mat salleh* in Malaysia, and *villaiti* in India. Japan closed its shores to foreigners for a century or more. In India, it was considered an act of contamination by the high caste Hindus to go abroad. Nepal was officially opened to tourism as late as 1955. Bhutan allows in only 2000–3000 tourists a year.

Colonialism also profoundly influenced, for better or for worse, Asia's economic and political institutions. Asian views of the role of foreign investment, multinationals, the World Bank, the International Monetary Fund, and economic and political pressures often accompanying loans and aid is best understood in the light of their colonial memory.

The influence of history on the thinking of Asians is not limited to the colonial past. Many ancient beliefs still play a decisive part. These stem from the cherished, if often romanticised, past: China as the middle kingdom, India's Ram Rajya, Malaysia's Melaka Sultanate, Korea's Hermit Kingdom, and Thailand's Sukothai. Asia's past holds its present in a tight embrace. Modern life continues to be judged by old values, creating a complexity of behaviour in Asians that foreign colleagues often find baffling. For example, Japanese managers are the products of both an ancient society and a modern economic miracle. They are willing catalysts of change and yet seem to be forever searching for the still centre of the universe. In India, almost every modern act is judged by old values as if centuries of Moghul and British rules were momentary aberrations. Despite Mao and the cultural revolution, an average Chinese still abides by the tenets of Confucianism.

Language, another powerful cultural factor, is closely woven into the fabric of Asian societies. Asian managers recognise the importance of English as a business language, but dislike it to be used as the most important criterion for promotion. Nor should one become a fanatic about its use in the office.

The family is still the dominant social and spiritual force in Asia. Motivation to succeed at work often derives from family pride and family needs. Caring for aged parents, helping younger brothers and sisters, and enhancing the family name are overridingly important. These influences cannot be separated from considerations of career advancement. Countries with a family-centred orientation are sometimes called 'contact societies' and are different from countries where individual privacy is never broken without invitation. This has an important bearing on how multinational managers should approach their colleagues.

Universal values

These cultural forces also determine how Asians view many universal values. Loyalty, for example, is more narrowly defined as an obligation to one's family, clan, village, or social group. Asians live in a complicated web of kinship ties based on a concept of mutual obligation. Respect for one's elders is a key element in this relationship. *Inhwa*, an important principle of Korean business behaviour, means harmony between unequals in rank, prestige, and power. It derives inspiration from the Confucian ideal of total loyalty to parents and authority figures. The concept of duty lays emphasis on submerging oneself as a member of a group. The Japanese concept of *wa*, which also translates as harmony, calls for mutual cooperation to devote the combined energies of all individuals towards achieving the goals of a group or a company.

Contentment, which is sometimes confused by expatriates with a lack of ambition, has two aspects in Asia: social and individual. One is taught to be content with life. 'There are fish in the waters and rice in the fields', goes a Thai saying. In other words, don't worry as no one will starve. On an individual level, while self-fulfilment is highly rated in the West, it is often merged by Asians (at least philosophically) with something higher than the self—with religious or spiritual pursuits. The notion that economic progress should lead to greater individual happiness is viewed as a Western concept. The Asian belief is that happiness comes from submerging one's self-interest in that of the group, such as the extended family, or by discovering it from within oneself.

Honour plays a critical role due to tradition and custom. This is frequently confused with losing face by people who do not understand its serious side. *Guanxi*, for example, (sometimes described as the Chinese old-boy network) is a relationship which binds parties together by the concept of face—meaning respect and honour. Losing face is like a tree stripped of its bark, a matter of life and death.

Justice is seen in its religious or metaphysical perspective rather than in its legalistic context. When something bad happens to a person who is viewed as evil, the Asian comment is, 'Well, justice is done.'

Traditional values

Managers must be seen as good people in order to be accepted by their subordinates. They must demonstrate a concern for their subordinates and protect their livelihood. V. Krishnamurthy, chairman of the Steel Authority of India, and the country's number one technocrat, stresses the importance of traditional roles: 'I come from a place where the entire village was owned by my family,' he says. 'The family was the nucleus. Everything else surrounded it. We didn't bother whether a person tilled the land or did something else. If there was a wedding at his place, we all took part. If he was sick, we would visit his home. I believe that all these things that are considered virtues have roots in our traditions.'

Traditional ways were changed due to the influence of the British, and later by American management education, he says:

> In the last thirty years the management education of this country
> has been based on Harvard case studies where the human side of
> management was subordinated to the material side. We tried to
> put a lot more emphasis on machines. We had extensive data about
> machines, about parts and maintenance. But when it came to human
> beings who are a long-term fixed asset, there was a lack of awareness
> that we must keep them continually updated. After all, you can buy the
> best of machines, the best of technology, but eventually a motivated
> group of people are going to deliver the goods. That thing was lost sight
> of.

By his own example, Krishnamurthy is fostering a greater people–awareness among the country's managers:

> Even now our formal management education lays comparatively less
> stress on the human side than on other sides of business. But over
> a period of time now, there is a movement in Indian management urging
> that this has to be taken care of. There is actually a group of us who are
> working today to propagate the message that productivity can come
> only through people.

Paron Israsena, president of Siam Cement Group, Thailand's largest and most prestigious industrial conglomerate, and chairman of the Federation of Thai Industries, stresses that his company never fires any employee. Reflecting on Thai traditional values, he adds: 'When we work in a Thai company, those values are still there. But what I am worried about is that in twenty years when the new generation comes up we may lose a little bit. But we won't lose a whole lot, that's for sure. That's the Thai people. That's Buddhism.' He hands me a copy of his company's code of ethics, saying, 'We believe in being good people, morally good. We believe in righteousness. I'd like you to read this—our code of ethics I published for our employees. You read the introduction. That's Thai, *real* Thai.' I asked if he is strict in judging the competence of people. Not surprisingly the answer was typically Thai. 'We take the middle road like Lord Buddha said. We are not too strict and we are not too lenient. We take the middle road.'

Gaston Ortigas, former Dean of the Asian Institute of Management, highlights two Filipino traits which easily apply almost anywhere in Asia. 'One is *pakikisama* which is like getting along with other people (smooth inter-personal relations) as a very important value. The other is the idea of *utang na loob* which means having a debt of honour (literally speaking, a debt inside), some obligation that you recognise because of something that the other person did for you at some time.'

He stresses that Filipinos who went to business schools in the USA lost these traits to a substantial degree. I asked if modern management as taught by foreign business schools suppresses our cultures. 'It does, it does, it does,' he said repeatedly. People are now looking at the old idea of *pakikisama* more closely, he added. 'Now they are trying to understand it from a management point of view and not just so much as goodwill and knowing how to get along. A deeper idea which means *pagkatao* (personhood), and which is more comprehensive, is taking shape. Depending on who is using it, some people will say it really means dignity.'

Most of what Ortigas says about the Filipino manager is generally true of the whole region. 'Initially the biggest advantage was to have worked for a large international company. One could access the developments in management much more quickly,' he explains. 'But that was enriched in the late 1970s when people began to understand important things about their country in their own language. They began to enrich and deepen their sense of management in this part of the world. I think this is the excitement that's going on now, particularly among younger people who are starting to emerge.'

The search for an identity

Asian managers' search for cultural identity is part of a much bigger scene. Greater economic and social development is making people raise many questions about who they are and where they want to go. Half the workers in Singapore, for instance, are employed by about 700 foreign companies. Together they produce 70 per cent of the total manufacturing output. American corporations with local manufacturing operations share more than half of Singapore's exports to the USA. But not long ago Prime Minister Lee Kuan Yew warned that Singapore risks becoming a pseudo-Western society due to its mostly English-language schools unless parents pass on basic Asian values to their children. So far, only some in the top layer of society had lost their roots, he said. 'Only the highly educated have that degree of biculturalism where they are more Western than Eastern. In the middle and the lower ranges, it's still very much an Asian society.'

However, an almost imperceptible change in Singaporeans had preoccupied him for some time, Lee told university students. 'The Western habits—songs, dances, whether it is disco or Swing Singapore, or dress styles, or fast-food—that's just a veneer,' he said. 'But if it seeps down, if we are not conscious of what is happening to us and we allow this process to go on unchecked, then I believe we will have a bigger problem to deal with, where the middle ranges will also be more Western than Asian. The problem is going to be acute over the next ten to fifteen years.'

Many Singaporeans have expressed similar views in the readers' forum of the *Straits Times*: 'Even nowadays, *char kiak* (clogs) are still widely worn by many Japanese during traditional ceremonies or occasions,' says one reader. 'Japan is such an advanced country but it still keeps its traditions and culture. Why can't Chinese Singaporeans learn a bit from the Japanese? Being a Singaporean or being English-educated does not mean one has to discard one's own traditions or culture. This is why I respect the Malay and Indian Singaporeans. Although educated in English, they are proud of their traditions and culture.'

The Japanese themselves are earnest in pursuing *kokusaika* (internationalisation). They are quite keen to buy fashionable foreign brands and are becoming more open to overseas influence. Yet at the same time, Japan retains its deep cultural values. Children of Japanese executives assigned abroad are often sent to special classes on their return to be re-oriented into the Japanese way of life which does not brook the degree of individuality to which they become accustomed overseas.

The yearning for national identity in the Philippines is dramatically expressed in a report by the Philippine Senate. Called the 'Moral Recovery Program', the report laments that the Filipino culture 'is not built around a deep core...the colonial mentality is manifested in the alienation of the elite from their roots and from the masses.' There is a 'basic feeling of national inferiority that makes it difficult for Filipinos to relate as equals to Westerners.' Even the simple choice of language weakens the Filipino. 'Using a foreign language [English] which foreigners can really handle better leads to an inferiority complex...at a very early age we find our self-esteem depends on the mastery of something foreign,' the report states. Almost in desperation, it suggests several remedial measures including wearing and using only Filipino clothes and products one day a year, banning foreign TV ads, re-telling of town or community history by old folks at public gatherings, and Philippinising the entire educational system. Such sentiments epitomise the deep-rooted sense of cultural loss Asians feel from centuries of colonialism. An American friend once told me how he had learned to get on with his Asian associates. 'Now,' he said, 'I always try to understand where a fellow is coming from.' He meant not only the person's background experience but also the impact of history on their particular attitudes and values. Because of history, he found people could disagree with you without being simply perverse.

From a historical viewpoint, even ideas such as a broader Asia-Pacific economic collaborative can look like a ploy by rich countries to hijack Southeast Asia's newly-won prosperity. It revives fears of losing one's soul in a bigger conglomeration. It is an undefined anxiety that resides in Asia's genes, a free-floating fear on the sea of memory. It is the recollection of childhood encounters with strange soldiers toting long rifles. It is recalling the hurt and humiliation of being thrown out of a railway compartment, barred from a recreation club, and denied access to the hilltop of your own hometown.

Ironically, it began partly on the premise of saving souls. Ferdinand Magellan planted the cross on the shores of the Philippines in 1521. But with each imperial venture, the conquest for God gave way rapidly to a quest for gold. Could history not repeat itself, in the name of cooperation this time? After all, it happened under even the most recent and enlightened of foreign rules. In his book *In our Image*, Stanley Karnow, a former *Time* magazine correspondent, presents a disturbing account of America's empire in the Philippines. After 300 years of medieval Spanish dominion, the modern Americans came. By 1910, twelve years after Commodore Dewey blasted the *hidalgos* in Manila Bay, more Filipinos could read and write English than any other language. However, 'patriotic' history lessons included George Washington's cherry tree and Paul Revere's midnight ride. An American primer taught that 'A is for apple,' a thing foreign to Filipinos, and pictured John and Mary amid alien snow. While a noted Presbyterian minister scorned the 'novel idea that the reign of Jesus is to be widened under the protection of shells and dynamite,' American forces had killed some 20 000 Filipinos who resisted. About 200 000 civilians died. The countryside was devastated. The number of *carabao*—water buffalo, the rice farmer's mainstay—shrank by 90 per cent.

There is a persistent fear in China as to whether modern ways of life will bring about the destruction of cultural essence. Says Dr Michael Bond of the psychology department of the Chinese University of Hong Kong: 'They have the legacy of 4000 years of civilisation and a concern about the impetus of an Industrial Revolution which is not the product of their own country.' The university picked 40 traditional Chinese values to conduct a worldwide survey on people's views on them. These ranged from filial piety, humbleness, repayment of both the good and evil that another person caused you, chastity in women, having few desires, moderation, following the middle way, benevolent authority, and loyalty to superiors. The results showed that a belief in these values was shared by most other Asian countries.

Very little thought, however, is given to the sense of cultural identity in the corporate context. In fact, their identity is sometimes considered a drawback in Asian managers. At a seminar I attended in

Hong Kong, a successful American-Chinese executive of a fast-food company expressed concern that his Chinese-educated employees were reticent and would normally defer to Americans. He declared that he had asked his head office how they deal with minorities so that he could learn to manage the situation better in Hong Kong. One could not help wondering whether he realised that he was portraying as a 'minority' the people who form an overwhelming majority in the territory. They had to emulate foreigners to get on in their careers. They had to speak in a foreign language with a proper accent. At the same time, they had to cast off their diffidence and stop deferring decision-making to expatriates.

Considering that the seminar dealt with the emerging Asian manager's role in Asia's theatre of prosperity, the naiveté in evidence was stunning. It was all right to groom Asians for senior positions because they cost less, not because their future was rightfully theirs. Asian managers can be just as effective as expatriates provided they enjoy head-office support, explained one foreign participant. That support was necessary, the participant continued, because Asians generally prefer to work under a 'big white boss'.

Such remarks betrayed no awareness of insult. The fast-food executive at least camouflaged the servile attitude resulting from 150 years of colonial status by calling it 'cultural conditioning', innocently comparing the intercultural relationship to that of minorities and WASPs in the USA. But for the rest of the people taking part in the seminar, it was another stereotype monologue: expatriates debating with other expatriates about how to shape the Asian manager's destiny. That seminar was a microcosm of the conflict between the corporate and the cultural worlds that both Asian managers like Jaye Shagun and thousands of multinational managers face in Asia every day.

3   Value systems in action

Jeremy Pickle, regional president of Westbig Corporation, and Jaye Shagun, a department manager, had worked together for a number of years. They have had differences of views on several occasions and each had felt an undercurrent of tension in their relationship. But Jaye was hardly prepared for the conversation that took place between them on Jeremy's last day at the office. Jeremy was returning home and though he was not given to making confessions, emotion and conscience got the better of him this time. As he went round to say his goodbyes, he stepped into Jaye's office. Here's their last conversation:

JP: Well, Jaye, this is the hardest goodbye. I must make a confession before I go.

JS: Jeremy, we'll all miss you.

JP: I'm not too sure of that. But I'll remember a lot about you. You know as well as I do that we did not always see eye to eye with each other. What I have secretly admired about you is your ability to survive as a person. I tried to break you many times but always failed.

JS: Well, that's pretty frank, Jeremy! I was never sure whether you admired that trait or resented it. Personally, I have always thought highly of your intellectual ability. But I have also wondered why you put down people so often. Unlike some other managers, I was never prepared to become a 'yes' man, but it did not mean that I did not respect you.

JP: You know, the problem was that you were always able to separate Jaye the man from Jaye the manager. And you expected me to do the same in my case. I know that many things such as your family pride and personal values are more important to you than career considerations. But you should not expect that from every person. Getting to the top is in itself a strong value. That's why I felt uneasy whenever we thought of your promotional prospects.

JS: What you are saying is that I refused to become a facsimile of my Caucasian counterparts. Don't you think it amounts to racial and social manipulation? Certainly there is enormous hypocrisy here in the name of corporate culture. Why don't you treat people as individuals?

JP: Well, that's a very fine tradition of Western liberal education. But you can't run a company with a bunch of highly individualistic people. You have to learn to wear a manager's mask. No one is saying that the mask should totally eclipse the man behind it. But one has to tame one's personality or largely submerge it in his job. How else does one measure a manager's worth?

JS: I'm not sure. It seems to me that a manager's position can never be bigger than the man. Making a living should be part of life, not life itself. All the world's functional expertise and professional competence cannot be a substitute for each man's search to be a complete man. Anyway I wish you all the best in your new assignment. Come back and see us sometime. Give our warmest regards to Jean and the kids.

It is hard for Jaye ever to forget that conversation. It inevitably brings back many memories. He recalls the time, for instance, when he and Ernesto had a meeting with Jeremy to discuss a proposal by the personnel department to discontinue the practice of staff carrying part of their annual leave forward to the following year. Jaye remembers that he had been very forceful, even a little emotional, in opposing the proposal. He had stressed that the policy would create resentment among local employees who would be unable to plan overseas holidays of a worthwhile length. But Ernesto had sat there watching Jeremy's expression for hints. He had finally expressed views conforming strictly to the objective of reducing long absences.

SHAMs and CRAMs

Jaye has always felt that Ernesto is a SHAM (Standard Hybridised Asian Manager). People like him are products of company management development programs designed to produce middle managers who fit in well with foreign supervisors. Often with foreign degrees, they go through training courses that develop effectiveness in marketing, accounting, or manufacturing. They adapt well and are steadily promoted to more important positions. Their dress and behaviour imitates that of foreign managers. They can look at their own countries with the same 'objective' perspective as do the expatriates. In short, they are perfect subordinates.

Jaye is, however, happy to see that SHAMs are gradually giving way to CRAMs (Culturally Responsive Asian Managers). This change is forced by more competition from national companies, better business education, greater complexities in the political and economic environment, and higher expectations of middle managers. Far-sighted multinationals are realising that Asian managers contributing their cultural knowledge and sensitivity can help meet market competition and so satisfy head office. They realise that without evolution of attitudes towards middle management, employees may either quit—taking with them years of valuable experience—or serve as demotivating role models for younger staff. Or they may become SNAMs (Severely Nationalistic Asian Managers).

Jaye often thinks of his friend Akbar Ali. Educated in Pakistan, he was determined to outshine his colleagues with foreign degrees. He copied everything the expatriate managers did and ardently pursued training programs. Akbar, an exemplary SHAM, was picked for a developmental assignment as a business analyst at the company's regional office. He mastered the techniques in a very short time and was promoted. As a senior analyst, he felt for the first time he could make a more valuable contribution by being Asian. Transferred back as director of the local subsidiary, he found himself in an environment where he could help by pointing out ways for the company to develop a style more acceptable to Pakistanis.

Akbar tried to become a CRAM. But he was frustrated by his company's president, who frequently reminded him he was working for a foreign firm. Within two years Akbar was a SNAM. He finally accepted a position as chief executive of a national company in the same business. He now adapted to his own advantage every trick he had learned as a SHAM. Other employees joined him, and Akbar's company is now market leader in its product line. Top management at his former employer will never know the truth because Akbar was presented only as a disgruntled manager.

Obstacles to progressing from being a SHAM to becoming a CRAM can be removed even when they are embedded in the system. Training programs should focus on cultural differences as assets. Ability to use cultural factors to help formulate company strategy should count in determining performance and gauging potential. Plans for growth should be set in the context of national economies and not be dictated merely by global corporate policy.

The environment in most multinationals, however, continues to nurture SHAMs. It is reflected not only in their training programs but is also pervasive in their entire corporate approach. Even in their use of management consultancies, multinationals are frequently conditioned by this attitude. They often hire them to enable them to grind their corporate axe rather than for real advice. Take for example the use of the Hay Group's job-evaluation method by a well-known international company. The system is meant to ensure a fair comparison of jobs both within a single organisation and between different ones. By ascribing points for know-how, problem-solving, and accountability, each job is rated and given a score. In itself the system can be a just method of job classification. Though the methodology may sound simple, using it requires professional expertise and objectivity.

John Pitts was a salary-scale specialist with the Asian operations of an international company. He had had some training in doing job evaluations in the USA and was given that responsibility when he came to Asia. The company wanted to reassure managers that they were being treated fairly. Pitts borrowed a manual from the head office and set out to grade jobs. It was a disaster. Managers of Asian subsidiaries were up in arms. The way jobs had been rated simply endorsed the preconceived notions of the regional head office management. It did not take into account the special know-how and problem-solving skills required in many of the local markets. The prestige of a popular system had been used to give credence to a purely subjective exercise. I narrated this case to Claudio Belli, who was at the time vice-chairman of Hay Group. His response: 'Our system offers a technique and a discipline. But you don't hire a consultancy only for that. You use a consultancy for objectivity.' That is precisely what was lacking in the exercise conducted by Pitts. Lance Berger, executive vice-president for national compensation practice at the Hay Group's headquarters remarked, 'We do our best, but we can't be better than our clients. We do try to ward off the tendency to institutionalise stereotypes.' Little is being done, however, to address the problems unique to the Asian management situation. The vast majority of companies simply apply here techniques that were developed in response to practices or problems elsewhere.

Lapels and toothpicks

The SHAM conformity is often taken to a ridiculous extent, forcing Asian middle managers to become corporate clones not only in work but also in matters of dress and social etiquette. Though few top executives would admit to it, each office maintains its own unspoken dress code. Even a slight variation can mark a person as a manager of mediocre potential. The personal likes and dislikes of senior managers also play a critical part. Khun Bhanu, a Thai manager, recalls his shaky start with a foreign company. Fresh from an American university, he dressed impeccably according to the fashion of the day—broad tie, wide lapels, flared trousers, and platform-heeled shoes. He was assigned to the accounting and finance department under a man who detested trendy menswear. This man put up with Bhanu as long as he could, but his first formal assessment described his new charge as a flashy young blade who would never make it in the grind of the controller's duties. The matter of dress was never mentioned.

Another criterion that rarely appears on evaluation forms is social mannerism, breached at the cost of one's career. Vincent Chu had performed remarkably well as a manager in Malaysia. Then his company invited him to the regional head office in Hong Kong in order to give its senior executives a closer look at him before promoting him. Chu failed—but for reasons that had nothing to do with his managerial abilities. What ruled him out was his table manner. The executive vice president whose opinion counted most took Chu out to lunch and was completely put off by the way he waved his toothpick around while emphasising a point. Sad though it is that such trivial things can have such a devastating impact on one's career, even more tragic is the fact that the employee who is passed over almost never finds out the real reason behind his lack of advancement.

Most supervisors merely judge, and either don't have the courage to tell the 'victim' about a 'fault' they may have, or take it for granted that such matters are common knowledge. Yet these supervisors would never admit that it is so easy for their cultural prejudices to influence their judgments. Although some personal habits are universally disagreeable, other behaviour is objectionable only in specific cultures. Since standards of what is objectionable vary from culture to culture, it is obviously unfair to judge a person's behaviour solely on the basis of foreign etiquette.

Roses and greeting cards

The same is true of social customs. Asian managers are expected to follow Western norms even though they appear superficial compared with their own traditional ways. I am reminded of my friend Jambon whom I found in a foul mood on St Valentine's day last year. As a rule he doesn't repeat himself, but this time he sounded like a broken record. 'Why should anyone spend $10 on a single rose?' he kept asking. 'It's a complete rip-off, that's what it is.' Jambon is generous by nature, so obviously it wasn't the $10 that was bothering him. What he resented was being forced to honour a custom not his own. A few managers at his office had given flowers to their secretaries. Jambon held out, but by late afternoon he discovered that his own secretary had developed an unusually severe headache. Grudgingly he went out and bought one of the last roses in stock at the nearby florists. And therein lay the root of his wrath. Jambon then launched into a monologue on the injustice of simultaneously trying to keep up with Asian and Western observances. 'Where does it stop? A bottle of perfume on New Year's Eve, *laisee* at Lunar New Year and a big chocolate egg at Easter. He went on to list a series of occasions that in his opinion have turned private affections into commercial events, such as Father's Day and Mother's Day. The social pressure to conform with them, he complained, has taken away spontaneity and transformed feeling into false obligation and public display.

He mentioned his old boss, now retired in the USA. I knew he was very fond of him and his wife.

> You know something: his wife once reminded me about St Valentine's Day to make sure I would send flowers to my wife. I know she meant well. But think about it. It's a subtle form of socialisation in a company like mine. Your private life becomes an extension of your career. You end up doing things because everybody else does them, not because they are a part of you.

There was no stopping him now.

> How can they talk about the curious customs of the natives? Why should the dictates of commerce be more justified than something that has been a tradition for thousands of years? We are forsaking old conventions that provided a deep bond between husband and wife, parent and child, brother and sister. There is nothing wrong with the customs of Father's Day and St Valentine, but a card and a rose are a poor substitute for a genuine show of respect and love.

Dignity and modesty

The real issue, however, goes beyond dress, etiquette, and differences in social customs. It lies in finding a meaning in life according to one's cultural values. It's to do with preserving one's dignity and earning other people's respect. It concerns understanding the meaning of compassion. Jaye Shagun is admired by colleagues and friends as a person who has maintained his principles and humanity in the midst of the ruthless scramble for career advancement in his company. He is naturally unhappy when asked by management to offer early retirement to Chau whom he considers one of the best marketing managers in the organisation. The retirement age is 65 and Chau has just turned 50. 'They just hate to see people grow old, and yet they talk about team-building, loyalty, and morale. How can you achieve that if you openly victimise older employees?' he asks, clearly hurt. The problem lies in a basic attitudinal difference: old age is frequently equated with obsolescence by Westerners, but accorded honour and deference by Asians.

Rizalino Navarro, chairman of SGV & Co., the largest firm of chartered accountants in Southeast Asia, fears that foreign-educated Filipino managers are giving up too much of their cultural identity. 'We are too much attuned to the Western business approach,' he says. 'That is far removed from the more personal relationship-based management in Asia. We tend to be too competitive, too individual-oriented.' He believes that Filipino managers educated and trained in the USA often forget that their culture is quite different. And sometimes they even develop a notion that whatever quality is native to Filipinos is the wrong way of doing business. He is glad to see more emphasis being placed on the home culture as a basis for management. His verdict is that 'we should work with those elements rather than stray from them'.

Kim Duk Choong, executive counsellor of South Korea's Daewoo Industrial Company advises managers from developing countries to be more self-reliant. In helping to shape the economies of their countries they should avoid trying to copy directly from advanced-country models like those in the United States and Japan. 'While these examples merit study, foreign experience should be adapted to local conditions and local traditions,' he says. 'The economies of Taiwan, Singapore, and Korea, for example, are not copies of alien systems. Like the Japanese economy, they are unique.'

In a pioneering effort, the Malaysian Institute of Management organised three annual workshops on Malaysian managerial values. The country's cultural diversity presents a major challenge to its managers to find a synergy in the Malay, Chinese, and Indian values. At the second workshop, which I attended in 1989, the participants treated most cultural values as a shared heritage of Asia's old civilisations which could not be separated from modern management practices such as goal setting, employee counselling, and performance appraisals. They all held communication, consultation, and *mesyuarat* ('meeting') high on their list of priorities for managerial styles.

Tan Sri Hamzah Sendut, director of the ICI group of companies in Malaysia has a word of caution for Asian managers. 'Usually they either become Anglophiles or Americanised. That's all they know.' Even when they entertain distributors, 'it's not in the coffee shop but in the club.' He finds this artificial. Hamzah cites other examples of behaviour which could be adapted to the local setting. 'Let's take debt collection. Two years ago when times were bad, we were applying Western thinking to the problem. If a distributor hadn't paid within 60 days, our attitude was—let's have the shirt off his back. The company would send a letter, then a first warning, followed by a second and third warning, and finally a lawyer's letter. That's a very Western approach.'

Hamzah believes it is much better to ask a local director like himself to call on the distributor informally. Recourse to warning letters should be taken only when everything else has failed. Companies must demonstrate that they have a 'human heart'. To illustrate his point he cites the help ICI gave laid-off employees in setting up their own businesses. He praises Thai managers especially, because their first concern is for the people. 'Thai managers are very Thai. They are concerned that when you open an office you have a little prayer.' Hamzah acknowledges that 'we tend to forget sometimes. We argue that what it would cost to set aside a meditation room could be used for computers.' Hamzah adds, 'Sure we have a few managers in the company with Western attitudes. They are all well trained, well groomed and nice to talk to. But I felt that in managing a company that is becoming more Asianised, their Western qualities were somewhat artificial. I began to realise that for expatriates to be successful, they have to be sensitive to local culture, particularly in the context of the development of an Asia-Pacific trading area.' To be successful in that environment, Hamzah believes, a manager has to be multicultural and must respect other people's sensitivities.

Chanin Donavanik, executive director of the Dusit Thani Hotel Group, is the perfect embodiment of the Thai ideals of modesty and politeness. He does not follow blindly what he learned during his MBA studies at Boston University. He is a Thai, first and foremost. He forged his dream a long time ago on the playing fields of Chigwell in Essex when, as a 13–year old, he was the only foreign student in the school. 'People sometimes make fun of you, make fun of your country. Maybe that's inside me from that time. So I wish Thailand could be something better. That's why I'd like to see Thai hotels go abroad and compete in the world market.'

Corazon de la Paz, senior partner of Price Waterhouse in Manila, rates the values she learned from her parents far higher than influences from travel, training, or any mentor in the shaping of her career. 'We were four girls and from earliest years our parents were there to guide and motivate us, to teach us old values, the middle-class values of hard work,' she says. 'My parents were people who recognised the value of education. They felt that if there was nothing else they could leave us, a good education would be the greatest gift.' She adds, 'I don't know to what extent the things I do are Asian or Filipino and to what extent they are dictated by what I learned in my business school at Cornell, from Price Waterhouse, and from what I have observed as successful managerial practices.' Does she sometimes feel torn among such cross-currents? 'I would like to think there is a happy compromise. It shouldn't be business all the time. I know that I must relate to our people more closely, must be more understanding, listen more, and empathise more.'

Adaptability and roots

To many foreigners, the compromise appears to be no more than an incurable phobia about change. This is far from the truth. Take Prakash Tandon, the archetypal first generation modern Asian manager. Spending his childhood and adolescence in a series of small Indian towns in the early part of this century, he left for England to study accountancy when still a teenager. On his return, he rejected the prevailing practice of joining the civil service. Opting for industry, he eventually reached the top of the corporate ladder, becoming the first Indian chairman of the giant Hindustan Lever. In appearance and behaviour, Tandon was not much different from his British predecessors. But in a book he wrote about his life and times entitled *Punjabi Century 1857–1947*, he leaves no doubt that beneath the British accent and Savile Row suit endured a heart that was pure Punjabi. Despite enormous changes in his life, Tandon remained sentimental about his roots and early memories: farmer boys, love ballads, Punjabi food and festivals, folk songs, the *bhangra* dance, colourful weddings, and the sheer joy of the spring harvest. In *Punjabi Century*, his memory takes him back a thousand times to things eternal:

> The green rippling waves of wheat contrasted with the pure gold yellow of the mustard flowers—a sight I have felt the need to see every year, even if for a day. Like people returning to their mountains, valleys or seashore, I long to return to the Punjab to see its flat land clothed in its exuberant colours of growth; its many greens, the green of the chilli fields, the green of the wheat, of the gram and rice; and its yellows of mustard cotton and songra, the Punjabi flax.

The Asian manager is good in adapting but it would be a sad mistake to expect him to transform himself completely. Not long ago I was at a dinner party hosted by a friend, Gordon, who is the head of a foreign bank in Asia. He and his wife are gracious hosts, choosing their guests in a way that assures stimulating conversation. This night was no exception. As we retired to their drawing room for coffee, one guest popped a question as if on cue. 'Of all the Asians, who do you think are the most adaptable?' he asked, looking directly at me. Adaptable to what? I wondered. It turned out he meant to the ability to become Westernised. I was pre-empted by another guest who has lived in Asia for many years. 'Surely,' he said thoughtfully, 'the Chinese are the most adaptive.' Someone else chimed in: 'Of course, it all depends on which Chinese you mean. Personally, I'd pick Singaporean Chinese anytime. They can be assigned anywhere in the world and nobody would know the difference.'

An oil company executive cited the case of one of his young Hong Kong managers who had gone to the head office for a year's orientation. 'That was four years ago,' he said. 'He's so well liked they don't want him to return. He married an American woman and is settled there now.' These people, I thought, were not talking about adapting. They were talking about conversion, a process in which young middle managers become carbon copies of their foreign bosses. They wanted SHAMs not CRAMs. Though CRAMs are also good at adapting, they retain their cultural bearings and help their companies operate more effectively in the kaleidoscopic diversity of Asia. They are children of two worlds. As a rule, CRAMs understand Western culture far better than their Western counterparts know Asia. They are able to bridge the gulf between worlds so easily, to synthesise the two and adapt the best from each. They exhibit what biologists call heterosis: a tendency of cross-breed offspring to manifest qualities superior to those of both parents. This is true of many of Asia's outstanding managers. While mindful of their own history and traditional values, they are drawing on their cross-cultural knowledge to lay the groundwork for a promising future. Astute foreign investors are now beginning to recognise this as a priceless asset. But on the whole, it is disturbing to think how underrated good Asian managers still are. Why do companies continue to develop SHAMs when so many Asians offer a far better alternative?

Rejections and acceptances

There are many problems multinational managers face in coming to terms with the impact of local values on the behaviour of their colleagues. The first is that being expatriates, they develop 'international' standards which are often even higher than those in their own countries. They begin to expect and demand these standards everywhere.

Secondly is their tendency to be critical of practices in local societies which to them seem unethical, but at the same time to condone similar actions by their own companies. Asian managers find it difficult to separate personal and corporate behaviour. Top management at the Asian regional office of an international company once spent days in reviewing the case of its agent in Indonesia who habitually offered kick-backs to its customers. According to its Indonesian manager, however, the company ignored the more serious question of offshore maximisation of profit by maintaining artificially high transfer prices on its books. Though such an action was blessed with corporate respectability, the Indonesian manager found it no less reprehensible: it deprived Indonesia of its due share of taxes.

The distinction that expatriate managers are often able to make between personal morality and corporate conduct manifests itself in many other ways. Standards of truth and fairness are seemingly readily sacrificed in the name of business. Otherwise responsible managers absolve themselves because their unscrupulous acts are not committed by them as individuals. In the easy transformation of individual responsibility into corporate decision, they see no threat to social morality. I once met a manager who was visiting his company's Asian operations to finalise plans for sizable staff reductions. I expressed my surprise because, during a visit a couple of months earlier, the chairman of the company had made several statements that had indicated just the opposite. 'Surely you don't believe what chief executives say in public?' the manager asked me. 'But your chairman is no ordinary person. He's a celebrity in the business world,' I said. But the more I pressed the point, the less I was getting through. Quite clearly, this manager believed it was foolish to rely on what people say in their capacity as heads of business.

A third reason is that the strongest influence of values comes from old literature and folklore which is rarely read by foreign managers. The commandments of Confucius, for instance, are repeated in a million ways in books, plays, movies, and various other art forms. Precepts such as looking after one's family, keeping peace with neighbours, being economical with money, valuing education, and teaching young children the difference between right and wrong are very much a part of life. These are embodied by both fictional and legendary heroes. Tora-san, the main character in the world's longest movie series, is a reminder of compassion and concern for others at a time when many Japanese worry that modern prosperity is suppressing the quality of *ninjo*, or human feelings, central to personal relationships. These values are also the hallmark of cultured nobility. When Prince Hiro returned from Oxford after finishing his studies, he was asked about the qualities he expected in his future wife and empress of Japan. She must share his values, he said, including that of frugality. 'Someone who shops right and left at Tiffany's would not be appropriate.' While in the West each decade seems to spawn a whole new set of values and styles, especially for the younger generation, there is a greater feeling of permanence of values in Asia.

A fourth problem expatriate managers face in understanding the impact of local values on Asian colleagues is caused by their belief in scientific universality. Since technology honours no boundaries, managers with engineering backgrounds don't see the need to bother too much about cultural differences. This brings them in direct conflict with humanistic values. In his book *Technology and the Academics*, Lord Eric Ashby advises adopting

> ...the habit of apprehending a technology in its completeness: this is the essence of technological humanism, and this is what we should expect education in higher technology to achieve. I believe it could be achieved by making specialist studies the core around which are grouped liberal studies which are relevant to these specialist studies. But they must be relevant: the path to culture should be through a man's specialism, not by-passing it... A student who can weave his technology into the fabric of society can claim to have a liberal education; a student who cannot weave his technology into the fabric of sociey cannot claim even to be a good technologist.

A fifth drawback is the reliance by large companies on broad statements highlighting respect for differences in cultures but continuing their operations as single worldwide units. 'We value differences in gender, race nationality, culture personality, and style because diverse solutions, approaches, and structures are more likely to meet the needs of customers and achieve our business goals,' declares one such manifesto of a large international company. Since no change is suggested, it implies that the current practices reflect the ideal situation. Therefore, managers don't feel the need to make any special effort to understand local cultures.

Probably the best way to overcome these barriers is to consciously remind oneself that there are two sides to everything. Few managers can straddle two cultures as did Edwin Reischauer, the American ambassador to Japan from 1961 to 1966, was able to do. But it is helpful to remember his advice in his book *My Life Between Japan and America*: 'Quite unconsciously [I] had acquired the habit of looking at things two different ways—from the Japanese angle of vision as well as from our own national viewpoint. This...is the only hope I can see for world peace and human survival.' He could have added that this same faculty could make a critical difference between the success or failure of multinational managers today.

4 Leadership and motivation

Alan Seares, management committee member of Westbig Corporation's Asian operations, considered himself a born leader. His leadership style combined a technical grasp of managerial skills with a veneer of education. A short man, he was obsessed with power. His approach was based on what he called *qualitas*—something employees vaguely understood to mean excellence. But his most distinctive feature was the 'cultural' mastery he wielded over others. He often traced a link between his leadership style and ideas borrowed from literary works he had read. He believed these sanctioned his manipulation of people and his ever-increasing personal power. In reality, Sears was a monumental failure both as a leader and as a manager. He would often commend the Socratic method to subordinates, asking them to use questions and answers to challenge cherished assumptions through dialogue. But no one ever won a point with him in any discussion because he was totally convinced of his own superior knowledge. He would hire people promising them overseas careers in the wonderful world of Westbig even though he was fully aware of limited opportunities. He would often talk about great human qualities, but would judge the potential of middle managers from a narrow perspective conditioned by an emphasis on technical skills. In his long list of attributes for the future leaders of the company, there was no room for the virtues of compassion, patience, wisdom, humility, benevolence, and equanimity. And yet these are the very qualities extolled in Asian societies as inseparable from what is expected of the top people in most walks of life.

Sears would have enjoyed reading *The Classic Touch: Lessons in Leadership from Homer to Hemingway*, but would have certainly missed its message. Its authors, Clemens and Mayer, point out that great business leaders outshine others by their ability to persuade people to commit themselves to their highest levels of achievement. But they know that one cannot inspire that commitment simply by being proficient in the formulas and techniques of accounting, finance, and computers. The task requires an understanding of the human side of management. The book contends that leadership problems have changed little in the past 3000 years. The ancient Greeks, for instance, who sought to harmonise the needs of the individual and the group, have a lot to teach today's leaders. Agamemnon, in Homer's *Iliad*, is an arrogant and autocratic executive. He cares more about surpassing Achilles, the best warrior, than mobilising the hero's energies towards taking Troy. The results are disastrous. Achilles even considers going over to the other side. The lesson is that technical prowess in an organisation may be ineffective unless backed up by a strong bond between managers.

In Plutarch's *Lives*, the biography of Alexander the Great offers rich insight into the mind of one of history's greatest merger-and-acquisition specialists. Defying Aristotle's injunction to consider only Greeks as free men, he admired the Persians' organisational ability and insisted that his viceroys adopt local customs. In *King Lear*, Shakespeare examines an ageing executive's reluctance to surrender power and his flawed delegation and succession plans, while *Othello* shows what happens when a leader loses faith in his intuition and allows himself to be manipulated by those around him.

Whether or not one agrees with every interpretation in *The Classic Touch*, its broad message is clear: in solving our present-day problems, we instinctively see parallels with the past and try to draw lessons from our cultural heritage. The difficulty in managing in Asia arises when these lessons are based only on Western classics. Successful multinational managers realise that they must weave them together with local precepts. Unlike Seares, such managers lead by personal example. They know that it is pointless for leaders to talk about participative management if they are intolerant of other people's ideas. It is dishonest to paint a rosy picture of career prospects when openings for Asians for higher positions are scarce. And it is callous to applaud human qualities when in reality they don't matter one whit when it comes to promotion. Managers who say one thing and do another can never win the trust of employees. They only help to spread cynicism in the organisation.

Insight into the future

Great managers know how to rise above techniques, using these as mere tools. They win the commitment of others by making them share their vision of the future, not by a managerial faith in forecasting. Their decision-making is not merely a process of sifting through piles of information, but an act of faith based on keen insight. They are sceptical about the belief that if people could forecast accurately, they could manage well. They are more concerned about carving the kind of future they dream for their companies rather than waiting for others to forecast it. They are not overly enthused by terms like 'long-range strategic plans' which they consider poor devices to motivate people.

Many corporate strategic plans never get implemented, yet companies continue to devote thousands of managerial hours to developing them. The act of gathering information to prepare these plans acquires a symbolic value. Subordinates use it to reassure their superiors that a professional approach has been followed in recommending a particular course of action. But often selective data is presented merely to substantiate preconceived notions. The main purpose seems to be to enable senior managers to foster a sense of illusory control over the future. According to Steven Schnaars, author of *Megamistakes: Forecasting and the Myth of Rapid Technological Change*, nearly 80 per cent of business and product projections in the last three decades has been totally wrong. The world believed these dramatic prophecies because it is passionately seduced by technological wonder and overawed by the whole idea of change. But life is unlikely to be transformed drastically in the next two or three decades. Speculating on the future, Lee Iacocca, chairman of Chrysler, told *Fortune*, 'Looking twenty years out at what we will be making, there will be lots of changes, but we'll still have a car that is much the same as we see it today.'

Asian business leaders are far less obsessed with need for constant change than their counterparts in the West. Nor are they fond of using projections for the future as evidence of their pseudo-mastery over it. Their bond with their people is more in the nature of a shared intuition. In his book *The Intuitive Manager*, Roy Rowan makes a compelling case for the instinctive capacity which differentiates the true leader from an ordinary manager. 'Hunch' may be an odious word to the professional manager, but logic and analysis lead only part of the way down the path to a profitable decision. The last step frequently requires a daring intuitive leap. The enemies of intuition, explains Rowan, are big organisations that submerge the individual. Intimidating business organisations kill individual resourcefulness by demanding lock-step compliance. He adds, 'We need more MBIs (Masters of Business Intuition), not MBAs!' It is the element of conformity to prescribed processes and techniques (which Roy Navarro of SGV calls the step one, step two, and step three approach) that denies intuition any place in decision-making.

Take, for example, the Kepner Tregoe Problem Solving and Decision Making Program, to which managers of many large companies are routinely nominated. They proudly return with a plastic card depicting the 'ideal' decision-making diagram. But many of them merely play at being 'rational' managers. Any trace of their natural intuition is frowned upon as being unprofessional. Logic demands the right to smother a hunch. But 'logical' choices which ignore cultural factors and the intuition of senior Asian executives often prove disastrous.

A harmonious relationship

In the absence of a bond of mutual understanding, Asian managers are often reluctant to share their intuitions with others. In most large organisations the bosses are usually constrained to behave in a very formal manner that precludes close relationships. They consider distance a mark of seniority. The higher they rise, the more formal they become. Most managers worth their swivel chairs will insist that the surest way to weaken authority is to let their guard down. They firmly believe that familiarity breeds slackness and a lack of respect, and that sternness is the only way to maintain discipline. Their rank-consciousness makes many executives wary of mixing informally with their subordinates. They don't realise that they are living in the past. The Asian managerial profile has changed radically in the last three to four decades. The cosy days when class and courtly manners were tickets to the top have all but disappeared. Only a few senior managers are natural leaders who know that the art of institution-building is not confined to the office—that team spirit is rarely developed by formal exhortations at annual meetings. Smart leaders can work wonders of morale-boosting with a simple informal evening, at the same time ensuring they are not insulated from their staff.

Relationships developed during these informal gatherings encourage one's peers and subordinates to be open with their views. Only a few Asian managers would feel comfortable in expressing opinions diametrically opposed to their bosses' thinking in a formal context. But once a foundation has been laid through good fellowship, they will be forthcoming with their ideas, informally.

Ideally, expatriate managers must try to forge working relationships of perfect harmony with others, particularly with their deputies. The relationship between Bill, managing director of the Malaysian operations of an international company, and Ahmad, his second in command, is a good example. In many other cases, personal warmth cools under the pressures of the job, or when dedication to a career overshadows loyalty to a friend and colleague. But in the case of Bill and Ahmad, the bond is founded on the way they perceive their personal relationship. To them this is more important than implied by its cold and formal job description. As defined by their head office, Bill is in charge of the local operation, and Ahmad's task is to support him in the execution of his responsibilities, especially in areas designated by his superior. It is a standard 'one-over-one' situation. It recognises that two heads are better than one, but gives the top man the last word, while the number two man plays 'second fiddle'. These executives, however, have evolved a mutual pact that transcends traditional divisions. Ahmad clearly has a primary responsibility in personnel, finance, marketing, and community and government relations. Bill concentrates on manufacturing and quality control.

Each has a deep understanding of the other, derived from many a long talk. Bill is quite ambitious, but is also a devoted family man who spends as much time as he can with his two teenage children. Before coming to Malaysia, he ran one of the company's largest plants in the USA with a fine reputation—of which he is justly proud—for safety, productivity, and quality control. He is happy with his steady career progression. By contrast, Ahmad's 20–year career with the company, mainly in marketing, has been far from smooth. He has seen six changes at the top and has had to work with men who have had little grasp of the local situation. He has never forgotten the day during his first year when a number of employees left the office early during an outbreak of intercommunal disturbances to get home safely. They were confronted in the lift lobby by the managing director shouting, 'I've never seen a lazier bunch of people; any excuse to shirk work!' A later MD similarly lost his cool during a meeting when a Malaysian manager made a pointed remark. 'Look here, boy,' he said sharply, cigar still in his mouth. 'I may be new here, but I've dealt with hundreds like you in my time.' Ahmad was shocked. The company was going through a period of poor relations with government and many employees felt uneasy about it. All along he had felt things could be improved with more understanding of local sensitivities.

Bill realises that Ahmad bears the burden of recollections of this sort of treatment, and respects him for rising above the past. It would have been easy for him to conclude that Ahmad carried 'a chip on his shoulder', as another MD had once put it. Each admires the personal qualities in the other, not mere functional competence. They talk about things besides business. Although Bill is not religious, he practices the golden rule, 'do unto others as you would have them do unto you.' Ahmad's faith governs his way of life, and when Bill's daughter was gravely ill, he offered daily prayers and moral comfort to Bill and his wife. It is something they will always remember with gratitude.

Thus the relationship between Bill and Ahmad is not based on the kind of superficial adjustments popular with management psychologists. It derives instead from qualities which are essential for effective leadership: a respect for human values and a recognition for the need for self-esteem. It has become commonplace for an executive placed in a new position of power to replace his immediate associates because 'the chemistry is wrong'—a wilful indulgence of personal likes and dislikes that is widely tolerated, even encouraged. But two heads cannot be better than one if both think alike. Bill and Ahmad are a successful and effective team because they bring different strengths to the task of managing, each relying on the other's unique expertise. That indeed is the essence of true leadership.

The megalomaniac manager

The worst kind of leader is the megalomaniac manager. This godzilla of the executive suite eats everything smaller than himself. No predator of brute force, he uses cunning and intrigue to destroy people. He employs grandiose business schemes as pet projects to make co-workers look like lesser mortals. He scorns subordinates as weak and ineffectual, sacrificing them to the greater glory of the corporation. In his mania for self-exaltation, he scoffs at people with principles. He prizes change for its own sake, thriving on machination, and does not flinch at turning one colleague against another. To gratify his infantile sense of his own omnipotence, he instils fear. In short, he is the consummate corporate politician.

One such megalo-manager recently slithered his way to near the top of a company that wanted to corner the world market in a hurry. His first act was to proceed on a whirlwind tour of the offices overseas. He had been to Asia before and was greatly struck by the contrast between his childhood picture of the colonial continent and the reality of prospering Asia today. He had heard the twenty-first century described as the 'pacific century'. Now he saw for himself a mega-market with untold profit potential. But more important, he perceived a ready-made opportunity to hoist his career to new heights. Soon after his return, three managers from the company's Asian operations received summonses to the head office. They were presented with a plan that essentially negated every single marketing strategy the company had pursued to date in successfully carving out its niche in Asia. The gist of the mega-message was to double profits and market share in the next two years. The seniormost manager protested strongly. The market, he argued, had to be built up step by step. Too drastic a change would damage the company's credibility. The new plan called for too many people in product distribution, he warned, and threatened to destroy the continuity of his management team, a vital factor in Asia. This manager now does not have a job. He has lived in Asia for ten years and is understandably proud of his achievements with the company. He is no politician, and his main concern is about his departure's effect on the team he has struggled to build. He is not the type of man to run things by harsh fiat. He has tried to build his team cooperatively, infusing newcomers with a spirit of shared goals. All this, he fears, may now fall apart.

The danger of the megalomaniac leader is that his style soon starts percolating through the ranks. Young people who join the business begin to view success as the fruit of manipulation rather than honest hard work. They lose sight of the need for personal decency and principles, and fall prey to the mega-delusion of our times: that happiness is achieved only by abandoning conscience and selling one's soul.

Honesty

Above all, people expect honesty from their leaders. In this respect, Asians are no different from Western employees. In *The Leadership Challenge: How to get Extraordinary Things Done in Organisations*, authors James Kouzes and Barry Posner put honesty top on the list of what followers expect from their leaders. Over six years they asked more than 7500 managers throughout the USA to tell them what quality they look for or admire in their leaders. In every survey they conducted, honesty was selected more often than any other leadership characteristic. In a ranking of attributes such as competence, vision, being able to inspire, intelligence, imagination, and being caring, 87 per cent of managers selected honesty as the most valuable quality.

How do the followers measure something as subjective as honesty? The authors found through their studies that it was the leader's behaviour that provided the evidence. 'Whatever leaders may say about their integrity, honesty, and ethical practices, constituents judge leaders by their deeds.' They point out that leaders are considered honest when they do what they say they are going to do. 'Agreements not followed through, cover-ups, and inconsistencies between word and deed are all indicators of a lack of honesty. On the other hand, if a leader behaves in ways consistent with his or her stated values and beliefs, we can entrust to that person our careers, our security, even our lives.'

Sadly, words and action are at variance far too often. Multinational managers in Asia are often prone to rhetoric about the importance of the region to the growth plans of the company. They are the first to cite the century-old prophecy of John Hay, the American statesman: 'The Mediterranean is the sea of the past, the Atlantic is the ocean of the present, and the Pacific is the ocean of the future.' The statement sounds impressive. But when it comes to backing it up with investment plans at the head office, these managers usually lack the necessary conviction. And yet big business opportunities in Asia today lie in tapping into the explosive growth. It is often said that leaders are created as much by their context as by their individual talent and gift to design the future. The opportunities are everywhere before us. Even ordinary qualities should suffice for leaders to hoist honest people into effective leadership roles. Managers assigned to Asia for a period of two to three years, however, are simply unable to think long term. This distorts the natural organisational hierarchy in which one-day-time-frame workers are at the bottom and the vice president with responsibility to plan for three to five years is at the top. In between, the positions of foreman, manager, and general manager are graded on the basis of their capability to handle progressively longer time-frames. Asian managers feel frustrated because the time-frame of their expatriate colleagues holding senior positions is invariably shorter than their own. Thus the atmosphere in these organisations is characterised by a distinct lack of vision.

Complementary leadership

One of the most important tasks of senior executives in the current environment in Asia is to develop complementary leadership at the managerial levels below them. Without such institutional leadership, no organisation can look forward to sustained success. Unfortunatley, a majority of multinational managers are task-oriented and have little experience in developing institutional leadership. They are managers of strategy, not leaders of people. They know how to administer and control, not to innovate and trust. They rely on systems rather than on people.

Westbig's Asian regional office presented exactly that type of environment when Uncle Tim took over from Jeremy Pickle. Under Pickle people always felt they were working as 'hired hands', not as group members. They felt no sense of consistency between the company's goals and their own aspirations. But most importantly, there were no leaders in the organisation. At the staff meeting to welcome the new regional president, Pickle gave a breezy run-down of his successor's career in other parts of the world, adding patronisingly that the company had now decided to round out that experience with a stint in Asia. He disclosed—with something close to a sneer—that previous employees had given the new boss his nickname because of his grey hair. Moving up to the microphone, Uncle Tim declared that people were the main business of a manager. He revealed that he had already told the employee relations manager that he would be giving priority to people—to management development, training, and morale. His mission was to develop managers who could lead the company to realise its destiny in the coming pacific century. The employees listened intently, glancing over at the ER manager, one of the most unpopular members of Jeremy Pickle's team. Uncle Tim continued, 'These things are far too important to be left to Employee Relations. Senior management must be closely involved.' His remarks were amply vindicated in the months and years to follow. He always stressed that the company could not hope to make the most of growth opportunities if it did not accelerate management development for Asian employees. And since he was committed to growth, career development plans were set up for all promising staff. In a matter of three years, Asian managers were groomed to take over from expatriate managers in a majority of the company's affiliates in the region. Sales went up by 50 per cent. Return on investment was the highest among all regional operations of the company worldwide. Morale was high as Uncle Tim not only enjoyed the confidence of head office but totally identified himself with the region. Unlike Pickle, he was never seen as a passive spokesman for head office.

The dual approach

Multinational managers who aspire to be true leaders must learn how to practice dual management, reminiscent of a style of swordsmanship developed by Mushashi Miyamoto, a seventeenth-century samurai. Called *nitoryu*, it is the art of handling two swords—one long and the other short—and knowing which one to use when. Matsuoka Toshio, the Tokyo representative of the corporate planning office of the Matsushita Electric Trading Company, drew this analogy for me some time ago: 'Like Mushashi, an international manager also needs two approaches to deal with the two cultures in which he operates.'

Supporting this view, Miyoshi Yo, president of the HB Fuller Japan Company says, 'When I discuss something with the head office in the United States, I try to be Westernised. But when I deal with people in the company here, I am Oriental or Japanese.' Miyoshi believes that, though Asian management styles are greatly influenced by Western techniques, they are unlikely to undergo a complete transformation. 'The Western ways of management will gain strength and Japanese traditional ways will be weakened. But I don't think the Western way of management will take over. As long as we are Japanese, the Japanese portion will remain,' he told me, suggesting that non-Japanese executives should also learn to wield two swords.

More recently, the concept was brought to mind again when I met Paron Israsena, president of the Siam Cement Group. Pleased about the opportunities his company offers to employees for management studies abroad, he is also proud of their deeply felt Thai values. In addition to listing leading foreign business schools where Siam Cement sends its people, he stresses that his company never forgets it is grooming Thai managers. 'We concentrate on Thai qualities and adapt the techniques and practices we learn from overseas education to the Thai situation,' he explains. Will some of the qualities such as *kreng chai* (consideration for the feelings and wishes of others) and *bunkhun* (reciprocating a favour) not be lost as his company becomes more international? 'Ah, a very good question!' he exclaims. 'We are born with *kreng chai* and *bunkhun*. They are inside our heart. But inevitably in the future the cultures from Europe and the USA will come in and mix. But we are not afraid that we will lose our values. The majority of Thai managers—more than 95 per cent—are typically Thai.'

Gaston Ortigas, until recently dean of the Manila-based Asian Institute of Management, also highlights Filipino traits beneath the Westernised exterior of most managers. Referring to the influence of overseas business schools on Filipino managers, he explains:

> It forces them to behave in the workplace in a way that is not normal.
> In the beginning this was supported by the belief that the drive and
> analytical discipline that came with education from the better schools of
> the USA made up for the lack of sensitivity for the human equation.
> That was up to the middle of 1970s. But as the schools in the
> Philippines also began developing, they fostered a kind of counter-
> culture.

Foreign-trained Filipino managers tended to be task-oriented while the workers they supervised were all people-oriented. Gradually, efforts were made to correct the situation by placing a greater emphasis on human relations.

International managers skilled in managing only in mono-cultures rarely succeed in leading a team made up of many nationalities. Large companies often believe that by simply assigning employees abroad they are providing an opportunity for them to develop a feel for foreign cultures. But the process is far from automatic. Expatriate managers are often surrounded by local managers who have been promoted largely because they have acquired the company's domi-nant home culture. Yet the expatriate managers cling to their own customs rather than making any effort to adapt to the local setting. One way to break this isolation is to ask one's colleagues how they would handle a particular problem in their own cultural framework. Flexibility is the key to winning in a multicultural environment. A courtesan once told Mushashi that the tonal richness of a lute came from the freedom of movement and relaxation at the end of the core.

'It's the same with people,' she advised. 'We must have flexibility. To be stiff and rigid is to be brittle and lacking in responsiveness.'

Heads of families

The preoccupation with larger-than-life business figures has fortunately not yet taken hold in Asia. The exploits of these personalities as exemplified by the business media are quite often irrelevant to the needs of Asian managers. The experiences of these 'cult' figures are far too foreign for anyone here to identify with them. Nor will the concepts presented in such books as the *Leadership Secrets of Attila the Hun* prove effective in modern Asia. Becoming a king by killing one's brother or earning a reputation for rape and pillage on a massive scale are hardly the leadership qualities we need today! Leading people by fear may work on a one-time emergency basis. But an environment in which subordinates are in a miasma of chronic fear and apprehension will finally eat away at the foundations of any organisation. People afraid of the unpredictable moods of a vengeful boss will not produce their best for long.

Nor are senior executives who aim to be thought of as super-humans among mere mortals respected for long. They suffer from a desperate need to force their opinions on others. Many are motivated by insecurity which results in a superior attitude. Since the style of leadership expresses one's innermost personality, managers who are well-adjusted and decent human beings will always prove to be better leaders than power-smitten maniacs. Good managers are promoters of cooperation rather than of personal competitiveness within the organisation. Concern for employees is always on the top of their list of values. They are acutely aware of the impact they have on others in the organisation. Above all they act and are accepted as heads of families in their respective organisations.

5   Hiring, training, and rewarding

Nowhere do multinational companies come into sharper conflict with local cultures than in the implementation of personnel policies. Designed at head office, these policies are meant to be applied universally. Hiring standards, reward systems, and management development practices are centrally defined and adhered to with little initiative by local managements. The personnel or human resources department is viewed by employees as a robot dispensing the edicts of the management of a monolithic organisation. Though this department has the greatest need to adapt to the local environment, most companies continue to be obsessed with the idea that the head office approach is also ideal for Bombay and Bangkok. They even bring in specialists to their Asian operations to make sure that these policies are adopted exactly as intended.

Hiring

The hiring practices of multinationals are all too often based on how well a person would fit in the organisation rather than his or her real ability to handle an assigned job. The other day I was a witness to the job interview of an applicant for a middle-management position in a large company. She faced a panel of two product-line executives and a functional department manager. It was clear to me straight away that interviewers and interviewee were poles apart in their understanding of what the exercise was all about. The woman under consideration came well armed with samples of her work and was most anxious to deliver a full, prepared scenario on what she could do in this new post. The interviewers, by contrast, were more eager to know about her than her work! Even though the norms of their own corporate culture were not entirely clear to these managers, they knew from experience what type of person adapted best. Pleasant personality and the ability to be a team player ranked as top qualities. Past performance was not considered crucial. Alas, none of these expatriates explained that to the applicant, who was used to running her own show in a small firm. They did not make it plain that the job opening involved a supporting role in a rather large cast and that her compatibility with the other employees was therefore the most important factor.

The hiring practices of such companies suffer from six main drawbacks. The first, based on the principle of 'ultimate potential', maintains that a good manager hires only those employees who seem to have the best prospect of eventually reaching at least vice-president level in the Asia-Pacific regional office, or department manager in the company's worldwide headquarters. Never mind that in the past 20 years this quixotic policy has not been borne out in the case of a single Asian employee; the companies continue to recruit as usual.

The second mistake, closely linked to the first, is a tendency to employ people whom senior management might like. Graduates of prestigious overseas universities are hired to sell fertilisers to illiterate farmers in developing countries when locally educated staffers could do a far better job. 'I was promised all-round executive training,' says Rashid who is an MBA from a top American business school, 'but all I have done in the past six months since I joined the company is to squat with the farmers and drink tea.' He plans to quit if nothing better materialises in the next six months. Family connections, social status, and competence in a sport favoured by members of top management are also important in this context. Years ago I knew an English manager who boasted of having the best cricket team of any company in the South Asian country where he worked. Staff selection in this company was based on simple criteria: if you had an overseas degree and played cricket for your school, you were in. In the past, large companies operated in a privileged environment. In today's competitive world, they can't afford to squander either their own investment in people or the scarce talent available in the countries in which they operate.

Thirdly is company prejudice against non-graduates. Many large companies view a simple school certificate with disdain. But a degree is just a piece of paper, insists Eugene Campos, executive vice-chairman of the Malaysian property group Bandaraya Development, who had started out by doing odd jobs. Then there is the example of Meynard Halili, who rose from a Philippine Airlines check-in clerk to international cargo sales manager before becoming president of a top Manila air-freight company, Aspac. 'Lack of degree is not a crime,' he says, 'but often a result of circumstances.' Not surprisingly, people like Campos and Halili rank a college education quite low on the list of desirable business credentials. Says Campos, 'All you need is common sense, honesty, and dedication.' Intelligence and hard work are qualifications close to Halili's heart. In his own company, three of the six top managers are non-graduates. Though they have clearly earned that reward, Halili admits that he may be using reverse discrimination. 'I have this prejudice that education is a hindrance to growth,' he says. 'It creates a special cast of mind that gets in the way of flexibility, a quality very important in business and in dealing with people.' While most people don't go quite that far, they take exception to the built-in bias which large companies have against non-degree holders. No one denies that higher education is worthwhile for its own sake. It broadens the mind and enriches the human experience. But most Asian billionaires would be quick to stress that other qualities are often more important in the business world.

In fourth place—at the opposite end of the spectrum—is a prejudice against young MBAs. Masters of Business Administration are accused of being arrogant, overly ambitious, and intolerant of colleagues with lesser education. They are suspected of having a naive sense of self-confidence out of keeping with their lack of experience. True, their education lays too much emphasis on financial analysis, control, planning, and problem-solving, and too little on people. But most of the prejudice comes from the USA where they are blamed, in part at least, for the uncertainty of financial markets, the fall in standards of business ethics, and the mania for mergers, takeovers, and buyouts. The fallout from all this prejudice could have a negative effect on the development of new managers in Asia. Business graduates come back from the USA to work for family concerns. Entrepreneurs start their own businesses. Many find employment with large international companies. They all add to Asia's pool of professional managers. The USA may be able to enjoy the luxury of running down its MBAs; Asia certainly cannot. We need thousands more to bring about a transformation of family-run companies into public corporations. We need them in higher management at Asian operations of international companies. Notwithstanding some glaring omissions in their foreign business education, these MBAs bring communications skills, self-confidence, the ability to plan, computer capability, a willingness to take on responsibility, and familiarity with new concepts of financial management.

The fifth mistake is to assume that everyone is ready to leave home and is anxious to take up an assignment in another country. Of course, being an international manager can be a lot of fun. The work is an interesting challenge and usually entails a move to a different country every couple of years. But as the years go by, rolling stones begin to yearn for a little moss. Doubts about nomadism start in simple ways—noticing small behavioural changes in one's spouse or children, for example. Gradually a deeper sense of displacement and loss of identity takes hold. Small wonder, then, that some managers resist forsaking a happy home for the life of a corporate wanderer.

Tarrin Nimmanahaeminda, 44, president and chief executive officer of Siam Commercial Bank, spent six years as a young man in the USA earning a bachelor's degree from Harvard and an MBA from Stanford. He then joined Citibank, working stints in New York, Manila, and Bangkok for four years. But at 29, he made a move that looked to be the quietus to a lively career. He joined a local bank, the oldest in Thailand. Says Tarrin, 'It wasn't too hard a choice. I was going to be posted abroad. I did not want an international banking career. I wanted to stay in Thailand and work for a Thai bank.' Today he can look back on that decision as the best he ever made. It took him only ten years to reach the top. He says his sense of achievement is far greater than it would have been with any foreign bank. Judging from the communicative, modern, and efficient team he has been able to build at Siam Commercial, one has the impression that people get more excitement and enjoy more rewards on their home ground than most expatriates could ever attain.

Sixth is the ugly practice of poaching. While large companies generally go for fresh graduates, there are a number of medium-sized newcomers to Asia who meet their needs simply by stealing staff from others. Even head-hunters are not immune. An old acquaintance who is thriving on the speciality of moving people from one company to another complains that the scene has acquired comic proportions: a rival not long ago shamelessly stole his best executive!

Far-sighted companies with a yearly intake of trainees and programs designed to move people along a career path should not have to scrounge for staff. 'There is a general shortage of qualified people,' complains the senior executive of a medium-sized company in the information industry. After some probing, he admits that in the five years since the company moved its Asian head office to the region, it has not hired a single trainee.

A few weeks before he sadly passed away, Eduardo Lichauco, a veteran Filipino manager, told me how important it was for companies to grow their own talent to foster a sense of shared values. He talked fondly of his long years with the Ayala Group in the Philippines. That sense of identity is rare in companies which believe that they can go out and hire a dozen superannuated hippies from diverse backgrounds to build a business for the future. They overestimate their prospects of forging a team from such material, even though their environments are far from conducive to the creation of bonds among employees.

Choosing a career

In such an environment, thousands of young Asians with fresh college degrees face the hard task every year of choosing a job or a career. There is little professional help to guide them. Consulting friends and relatives can be useful, but such pointers tend to be quite subjective. In the main, these young people are left to fend for themselves in taking a step of far-reaching consequences. Though overseas institutions do provide some help, it is not always relevant. Knowing the average starting salaries of jobs in America or Europe can be grossly misleading for young men and women setting out on a career in Asia. Nevertheless, in the absence of other, more pertinent, factors, the starting salary often becomes overridingly important. Foreign or local, however, few companies doing business in Asia can match unrealistic expectations without throwing their compensation policies to the wind.

So for someone seeking a job, what are the other key considerations? Ideally, it is determining that a job and its environment match your unique temperament and psychological needs. First you should be clear in your mind whether, on balance, you are cautious or venturesome. Is your self-esteem easily satisfied by working for a large, well-known company—or do you thrive in a climate of challenge and bold achievement? Crucial here is an understanding of what your self-esteem requires. Your ego may get a boost by impressing others with a large company's logo on your calling card. But the road often calls for compromises for which you may be unprepared. Some multinationals are run essentially by people of the same nationality as the company's founders. Being a lifetime outsider is not a particularly soul-satisfying role.

Are you the sort of person who would be happy moving one rung up the corporate ladder every two to three years? If so, make sure you have the patience and personality to stand out as a belonger. Promotion doesn't always lead to enhanced status and may only put you up on the pay scale. Alfred Tse, an investment adviser with a British merchant bank, was promoted, but quit three months later because he still shared the same bench with six people. 'It's a funny pyramid,' he explained. 'You may expand horizontally but vertical moves are scarce.' Maybe you're a young achiever in a hurry who wants to take hold of the world by its ears and give it a shake. Do you rebel at the prospect of conforming for the sake of comfort? In that case, look for the adventure of a smaller firm in a business or profession that offers the thrill of risk-taking and the chance of making your millions before you are 40. This has to be a conscious choice. It is no good joining a staid corporation and expecting it to be entrepreneurial, or signing up with a smaller company and wishing things were more dependable. But don't panic; such decisions are not irreversible. Colin Au, a Harvard Business School graduate, left Westbig after just two years. He joined a smaller Malaysian company and rose to a directorship in less time than it would have taken him to become a mere middle manager in Westbig. Then there is David

Kirkhope. When I last met him, he had come from Australia for a get-together of young presidents. Looking prosperous and buoyant, he wondered how he had stuck to his earlier job with a large company for so many years.

Orientation

After you have made your choice, you may find that your company has no orientation program to help you feel at home. Too many people walk into their new jobs and are left to fend for themselves. Pamela Chan had just moved across town to a firm of architects much larger than her old employer. It was a step up. But she had hardly been a week at her new job when she began wondering whether she had made the right choice. It wasn't the work. She just felt like a total stranger in a cold climate. A couple of colleagues, she found, had been there for several months and still couldn't put names to the faces of the firm's partners. Somehow she stayed on and is now a senior architect. 'Things haven't changed much since I joined three years ago,' she confided. 'Newcomers are still treated as outcasts.' Though Pamela vividly recalls her first lonely weeks, she is not in a position to turn things around. She does whatever she can when someone joins her group, but remains convinced that any proposal to management for a formal orientation program would fall on deaf ears. Her reluctance to raise the issue is in itself evidence of a management syle resistant to change. If the subject was brought up, very likely it would be ridiculed. After all, a partner might snort, its employees have survived ever since the company was founded half a century ago. Trendy ideas about pampering newcomers are unwelcome. The problem is that Pamela and those like her are not the up-from-the-ranks draughtsmen hired by the founders; she holds degrees in architecture from two of America's most distinguished universities. But her company has not woken up to the revolution that has overtaken the make-up of today's employee force.

Little could be worse for staff motivation. First impressions last a long time, and frigid treatment is a killer. A welcome, however, ought not to be so zealous as to become a form of indoctrination. Some programs, often lasting from one to three months, are meant not so much to acclimatise newcomers as to convert them to a creed, going so far as to glorify even shady chapters of corporate history. Management precepts are taught by rote and company practices are presented as sure passports to success. Subtlety is used to achieve uniformity even in dress and manners. 'This is our way of doing things,' is the mantra recited to initiates. They are besieged by the company logo on memo pads and pens, coffee cups and coasters, key-chains, and calculators. On the program's last day they all assemble attired in their new company ties. The boss gives a pep talk, and the rites are concluded.

What's really needed is a practical program designed not to brainwash but to integrate a new employee quickly. Some clearly designated person should be responsible for showing newcomers around and introducing them to both senior and junior staff. It is demoralising for staff to hear colleagues of three months' standing complain that they have not yet had the pleasure of shaking the chief's hand. Standard items to be handed over should include company identity card, calling cards, stationery, and old faithfuls in the way of reference books. Sessions should be arranged with the heads of main departments to provide an overall picture of the company structure. Don't leave it to the employees to find out by hit and miss such policies as what may go on the expense account. Best of all, prepare a booklet explaining all these 'tribal customs'. A welcoming lunch would provide the icing on the cake in making a new employee feel wanted. A prospering company, after all, is more than a house. It's a home.

Training

Some old-fashioned executives still believe that managers are born, not made. They refuse to accept that most successful companies today thrive on talents cultivated by training. They continue to put their faith in mavericks who prefer their own bag of management tricks. However, management practice can no longer be seen as an arcane art exempt from scrutiny. It must now be open and visible. Managers must be seen to be effective at the basic skills of analysing, planning, problem-solving, and people-handling. Merely to do your job well and outperform subordinates in most tasks is not good enough. The *how* is becoming as important as the *what*. It's the code of the golf course; hitting the ball 250 yards straight down the fairway may be a splendid feat, but you are unlikely to win much applause if your grip, stance, and swing are clumsy.

The size and complexity of business operations today have made training indispensable in most companies. No longer narrow courses in accountancy, salesmanship, or production, modern programs aim at grooming all-round executives by ranging across many fields of expertise. They focus not only on the company's current needs, but on challenges likely to arise as a result of growth and diversification. They play a key role in developing heirs to positions at the top. Filling vacancies in the hierarchy with hired guns from outside can be useful in a strategy of change, but it is demoralising as a routine practice. Proper training is crucial to promotion from within. The best way to teach people how to swim, runs a maxim dear to older managers, is to throw them into the water. Perhaps, but only up to a point. The school of hard knocks can prove far more expensive for a company than formal training. Also, corporate fitness can be seriously undermined if senior managers persist in falling back on the meagre skills they learned on lower rungs of the ladder. Each successive promotion should be backed up by an increased inventory of skills—from methods of immediate use on the job to the basics of supervision, communication, conference leadership, performance appraisal counselling, general accounting, and public speaking.

In short, training has to be a way of life. 'As technology and business styles are changing every day, training must be continuous,' says Ronald Ho, regional manufacturing services director for National Semiconductor. 'Otherwise,' adds Singapore-based Ho, 'you soon fall behind others. Companies that do not spend on training are very short-sighted.' Progressive firms salute this today as a creed. Says John Chong, head of the Malaysian office of the West German automation firm Festo Pneumatic, 'We believe in human resources development and the philosophy that a company cannot grow faster than its people.' At Festo, training is formally planned for the whole year in advance. At Interlock Industries in Wellington, New Zealand, continuous upgrading is promoted by Stuart Young, the executive chairman, as an essential part of corporate culture. Every manager attends at least one outside course a year (partly on his or her own time), besides a series of in-house study sessions on quality control and interpersonal skills such as attentive listening.

Many managers, having risen from within the ranks without any formal lessons, remain penny-wise and pound-foolish. It is wholly outside their understanding how even modest expenditures on entry-level or promotional training can be justified. 'We've managed without it so far,' says one. 'I'd rather spend the money on hiring an extra hand.' Mentally they still live in the early days of the Industrial Revolution when a fifteen-hour working day was the standard by which productivity was measured, and more hands automatically equalled greater output. Fortunately, they are being overtaken by more far-sighted bosses. Festo's Chong, for instance, provides fourteen days' training a year to each employee. At National Semiconductor, Ho sets aside about 2 per cent of payroll costs for training. Interlock chairman Young is convinced that staff instruction has as integral a part in budgets as does marketing and advertising.

Unfortunately, most of the available training programs have a Western bias and totally overlook the cultural characteristics ingrained in people. A Thai manager for an international company got tired of his regional boss calling him an eastern potentate—which he would invariably do whenever he saw his secretary serving coffee on her knees. So when a franchised 'self-assertiveness' course was offered in Bangkok, the Thai executive sent his secretary along. A few days later, when the regional president was visiting again, the secretary asked him, 'Coffee, Bill?' The president was astonished at the change and was still talking about it when she came back with the coffee and got down on her knees to serve it!

Every week throughout the region, hundreds of employees are herded into conference rooms to be told how to speak, evaluate, plan, supervise, and sell in courses with names like 'Effective Negotiations' and 'Managing Organisational Change'. These programs certainly keep management happy and employees busy, but almost all of them are devised by Western experts for Western participants. On Asian employees the impact is superficial. There is no point sending employees to study something unrelated to the social and cultural environment in which they operate. Yet companies in Asia are besieged by agents from training consultants from the USA or Europe offering high-powered courses on every conceivable subject. One direct-mail flier, for example, exclaims, '. . . and that is why some of the most efficient and profitable companies in Europe regularly use this program for middle and senior managers.' The sole reference to Asia comes under 'foreign cultures'. Another brochure attempts to adapt to the local environment by using two large Chinese characters on the cover. They mean, it explains inside, 'crisis'. It then warns you that 'American organisations are living through turbulent years. We are facing a crisis of change.' There is no attempt to relate anything to Asia.

Training courses that ignore cultural differences invariably fail. Francis Martin, former president of the Bank of Canton, a subsidiary of Security Pacific, told me of a Los Angeles–designed effective salesmanship course for his Chinese senior staff. 'The fact the instructor was a woman may have had something to do with it, but there was no attempt at all to adapt the program to local circumstances.' John Newnam, Hong-Kong president of Drake Beam Morin, which specialises in career transition services, points out that some Asians will not actively participate in group discussions. Inexperienced instructors, misunderstanding this, may consequently 'being to train down'. Because large companies use training programs to introduce young employees to the corporate culture, adaptation to the Asian environment is important to prevent a sense of loss—of both individuality and national culture. Without this, companies may fail to promote a sense of partnership. Employees may accept corporate conformity and even some degree of manipulation in the name of organisational efficiency, but it is not necessary for them to feel they must renounce their cultural values.

To succeed, training programs must draw from Asian cultures

which have traditionally put great store in knowledge and wisdom. People with such qualities in centuries past were assured a place of honour. Some were even exalted as sages, their sayings preserved as signposts to proper behaviour. But today we tend to use old proverbs and precepts merely as reminders of lost standards and as sad reflections on contemporary lapses. While honouring the past, they are no longer considered as practical guides to living. Little has been done to tailor older wisdom to modern social needs. This omission is particularly striking in the field of human relations—dealing with acquaintances or friends, handling customers, and developing ties with colleagues.

Less traditional societies, especially that of the USA, have done more to 'modernise' enduring truths. Dale Carnegie's *How to Win Friends and Influence People* remains an outstanding example. The principles it expounds are all old, but they are applied to twentieth-century business. 'Don't complain about the snow on your neighbour's roof when your own doorstep is unclean,' Confucius said 2500 years ago. Carnegie turns that advice into one of his three basic techniques for treating business associates: avoid criticising others because it makes them defensive and determined to justify themselves. The other two also reflect insights of the ages: of all human cravings, the greatest is to be appreciated, and, secondly, the secret of success lies in the ability to see things from other people's points of view. Carnegie's abiding strength is that, like the wisdom it taps, his book relies not on mastering a set of tricks but on stressing the deeper need to change one's attitude and way of life. He reasons, for instance, that thousands of years of meditation on codes of ethics produced one paramount precept. By no means new, it's as old as history. Zoroaster taught it to his followers in Persia. Confucius and Lao-tse preached it in China. The Buddha and the sacred texts of Hinduism taught it in India. Jesus summed up the law, 'Do unto others as you would have them do unto you.' It is, after all, no good keeping golden rules in a museum. Their value is in the home, on the street, and in the workplace. In explaining one of his twelve ways of winning people over, Carnegie quotes from Lao-tse: 'The reason why rivers and seas receive the homage of a hundred mountain streams is that they keep below them.' This forms the basis of Carnegie's formula—let the other fellow think the idea is his. Carnegie's six paths to likability are based on similarly sound advice: become *genuinely* interested in other people; listen well and encourage others to talk about themselves; speak in terms of their interests; make them feel important (and do it sincerely); smile; and remember that a person's name is to them the sweetest, most important sound in any language. Of course, the hazard lies where sincerity is lacking. Herb Moser of Westbig Corporation, while briefly serving as acting head of Westbig in Asia, toured the office twice a day. Glancing furtively at the name plate on each desk, he would salute employees by name. 'Good morning, Josephine,' he sang out, and 'Morning, Mark,' as he breezed past—until the day the employees decided to swap name plates. Moser never found out why the office was so alive with merriment that day.

Finally, sending employees to the USA or Europe to attend management seminars is probably the least cost-effective method of providing training. Foreign management institutes who routinely call themselves international are often overwhelmingly European or American in their approach. Several years ago I attended an 'international' seminar at one such institute in Geneva. I was the only Asian. For the most part, European problems were addressed—references to Asia were superficial. The Swiss coordinator made the scope of discussion even narrower by introducing local issues. After two weeks of this I was left wondering what practical use there was in the exercise—and what was 'international' about it. Companies are not getting value for their money. It would be far wiser to hold high-level programs in Asia and invite experts to contribute a European or American perspective. Since Asian needs and levels of development are different, it would be far more effective to concentrate on issues that concern us directly. An important side benefit of such seminars is meeting other managers with similar problems. So unless a lot of Asians participate in these affairs, the value to Asians is minimal.

Rewarding

One of the big hurdles in effective multinational management consists of the differences in salaries and perks. When employees are classified as expatriates, third country nationals, and locals, it undermines all efforts to develop a truly multinational team. The salary system becomes manifestly unfair when a local employee replaces an expatriate. Even though the job remains at the same level, the compensation package usually drops by 65–75 per cent.

Yet these differences in salary become secondary when compared with perks which lend a special glamour to a manager's job. Gone are the days when an employer offering a pension scheme, provident fund, and medical plan was thought to be enlightened. Now even a prosaic list of perks covers a company car, club memberships, rent and utility bills, leave fare assistance, and children's school fees. All these make good sense in high-tax countries where living on perks is a way of life. But people crave them for more purposes than simply offsetting the tax bite. The more compelling reasons are the need to receive recognition, to build up self-esteem—and often just to experience the thrill of picking up the tab for an evening's outing with friends. Nigel Kwok was recently head-hunted in Hong Kong by a foreign company. Among the incentives on offer was a liberal expense account. Entertaining a few old associates, he shook with delight as he signed a sizable bill and announced, 'I am now a big spender!'

As modern Asian managers move up the ladder, they expect not only the customary bigger office and higher pay, but also the associated perks. More and more employers are finding out that money spent on perks can promote greater morale and productivity than a simple salary increase, which is often cancelled out by movement into a higher tax bracket. A chief executive of a communications company in Singapore told me that the decision to buy company cars for his department managers instilled far more pride than a comparable salary hike. 'Nobody sees the pay rise except the employees,' he said, 'but the company car is visible proof that you have arrived.' Membership in the local golf club puts one among the very top. All of this helps to create a general sense of well-being.

Bill Ho was recently lunching with a retired former colleague in a club once reserved for expatriates. Bill's company, Westbig Corporation, had been left holding club debentures because several expatriates had been transferred due to reorganisation. So Bill was offered a membership. His lunch partner had been a senior local employee back in the days when it was inconceivable to bestow membership on an Asian. Though modified a bit, company policies for expatriate and locally hired employees were still different, especially in terms of the perks given to the Westerners. Thus, notwithstanding the backhand circumstances, the simple fact of sitting in the club with his friend made Bill proud. The two recalled how expatriates used to be assigned offices with nice views while locals had windowless rooms half the size. The personnel manager then would never have relaxed the club-membership policy. Every time he circulated a memo it used to go separately to expatriate and local managers. That was when Jerey Pickle was president for Asian operations. Over lunch the two chuckled as they remembered how Pickle had discovered a designer to redecorate his office, catering to his ego with a desk nine feet wide. He used to put his feet up there while talking to subordinates. How the Asian managers disliked that.

From the management point of view, there is a serious problem with double standards in treating employees. Though the approach is becoming socially unacceptable, some foreign managers still come to Asia with outdated romantic expectations. A personnel manager told me of a young Belgian who had demanded a private pool in Hong Kong. 'Being selected for a foreign posting very often goes to these people's heads,' he said. 'They take it as a signal that their expertise is critically needed.' But competition is forcing head office to prune such incentives. In Hong Kong and Singapore, neither of which can be called posts of particular hardship, the fortunes spent on redecorating executive accommodation are hard to justify. Shareholders are becoming critical of opulent lifestyles for executives abroad, who are often difficult to reintegrate on their return.

Managers from Southeast Asia, whose countries are showpieces of economic success, resent the disparaging tag 'local'. Often with top-class degrees, they do not take kindly to being treated as second-class citizens. 'It's a pernicious system designed to make you feel diffident about your ability,' says one Asian manager. 'The longer you put up with it, the more you lose self-respect.' Says Tim Newton, an Australian who recently resigned from a large company to join a small one at home, 'You can't preach internationalisation of marketing and manufacturing and yet perpetuate an archaic employee compensation and benefits system.' Though he escaped the 'local' treatment, he had rankled at the 'third country national' classification for salary and benefits.

International companies must come to grips with this problem. It has an enormous impact on morale, sense of accomplishment, pride, and fair play. There is no easy solution since living-standard expectations differ and managerial salaries follow market trends. But the real issue does not concern salaries. It is the system of classification in the corporate hierarchy. It is a mystery how top managements of these companies fail to realise that in assigning them to a lower status, you are taking away the employees' pride. What's the point of investing huge sums in systems that divide so callously a company's most valuable asset? To be sure, a modern corporation is not a benevolent institution. But such clichés miss the point. The cost of club membership for Bill is 1 per cent of his salary, but it means more to him in terms of pride than can a greater remuneration. It says he is equal. For his company this is far more effective than all the speeches by management on team-building.

There are other ways too of motivating employees which do not cost a great deal of money. Ownership of stock by employees, frequently cited as the embodiment of democratic capitalism in the West, is almost universally ignored by business enterprises in Asia. In the USA a quarter of the 40 million corporate employees are enrolled in an employee stock-ownership plan. In West Germany, employee stock ownership is subsidised by government. In Britain, many companies have started experimenting with it. And stock options are going to a wider range of personnel. PepsiCo, for instance, grants them to almost all employees. Procter & Gamble last year announced plans to spend $1 billion on raising its ESOP from 14–20 per cent of outstanding equity.

How about holidays? A sacred ritual in the West, annual vacation is enjoyed by a relatively small minority in Asia. A privileged few may take several weeks off for sailing or skiing every year. But the majority take their leave bit by bit. By providing leave fare assistance or company cottages at holiday resorts, employers can help make well-earned recreation more meaningful for its middle managers. Also, it is iniquitous to grant people at the same level different durations of annual leave based on their nationality.

The impact of other schemes can often be improved by implementing them more imaginatively than is often the case at present. Most employers, for instance, seem to be satisfied with the basic minimum management of provident fund schemes. They leave the administration to someone in the human resources department who looks upon it as a dreadful chore. Nor is any employee representative included among the nominally constituted board of trustees. Most employees have no idea how the fund is invested. They never see a breakdown by categories such as stocks, currencies, cash deposits, bonds, or bullion. They have no idea how much of their savings are gambled on the bourses. A vast majority of employees are unaware that the amount invested in stocks by their investment managers can be as high as 80 per cent. It is important that both trustees and employees should be more closely involved in supervising the fund. The responsibility of trustees should not end with the appointment of a reputable investment management firm. They must periodically review the performance to satisfy themselves about the level of return and the security of investment. They must ensure that the investment managers present the review to employees at least once every quarter. It will be unwise to wait till the next market crash before giving employees some say in determining the risk and reward strategy for their savings.

Enlightened companies also have much to contribute to harmonious industrial relations. The attitude of some investors who favour introducing to their Asian subsidiaries a modicum of Europe's much-vaunted 'industrial democracy' is almost ancient. It is short-sighted to think that prosperity can be gained in Asia only by curbing a legitimate voice for labour. Discontent would only help sour the investment climate. It is particularly unwise for foreign investors to insist on barring unions from certain industries as a precondition for entry. Ironically, these same companies are now reconciled to unionists sitting on the boards of directors in their home countries. Threatening to dismiss workers who seek to organise is not the kind of statesmanship destined to foster a climate of cooperation and goodwill.

Asian countries can hardly insulate themselves from one of the most powerful movements of the industrial era. They only supply ammunition to unions in the West whose charges of 'cheap labour' and union-busting have helped restrict imports from Asia. Most foreign companies here provide decent wages and worker treatment. Why invite the charge of exploitation by resisting the emergence of responsible unions? The growing number of industrial workers with fair wages in their pockets have a purchasing power that is transforming domestic economies. To deny them a collective say on their safety, security, and welfare—to ignore them as mere 'dissidents'—is to risk alienating a potent market. The real social time-bomb is disaffected labour, not workers seeking democratic expression.

6   When development stops at forty

Several years ago, when Jeremy Pickle was assigned to Asia as the regional president of Westbig corporation, he delivered a stirring speech to the staff. 'The company believes in looking for the best talent anywhere in the world,' he declared. 'There is no reason why one of you should not replace me in time.' But older managers knew that the management development program of the company worked only up to a certain age and level. Beyond that limit it was unable or unwilling to fulfil the longer-term expectations it so readily generated, even encouraged, among young managers. The most the so-called high-potential employees could aspire to were the middle ranks. Their promotional prospects stopped when they reached forty. As time went by, it became clear that Pickle's statement was designed to further his own career rather than groom local managers to reach senior positions. Within a year he had picked a handful of young employees and promoted them to lower levels of middle management. Later, employees found out that it was all part of his plan to impress the president of the company who was scheduled to visit the region in the near future. Indeed, when the president arrived, the newly-promoted managers were lined up in Pickle's vast office like an inspection parade. Briefly, Pickle cited each person's achievements, as the president shook hands one by one. He told them that being asked to assemble in his office to meet the company's chief executive was proof that they had done well. They should be proud of their promotions and look forward to the future with confidence. It did not occur to Pickle that people may find it distasteful to be lined up like that or see it as a device to ingratiate himself with his superior. The incident is symptomatic of the three cardinal sins that characterise management development programs: patronising, platitudes, and promises. The lining up of young managers in this instance was patronising on Pickle's part.

Here's a statement that is pure platitude: 'I strongly believe that employees today have much higher expectations from their employers than they did 25 years ago. Meeting these expectations is a challenge.' The speaker is attempting to convey the subtle message that he is a perceptive observer of one of the great social phenomena of our times but is not unduly fazed by it. His words suggest that because he has been able to identify the trend, he can do something about it. The use of 'challenge' is meant to signify that his company has a positive attitude towards the development. What's far more likely is that he told his head office that—before his arrival on the scene—the subsidiary had hired too many MBAs and PhDs. It's a headache to keep them motivated. These employees know that international companies, due to their size and resources, are able to attract the most talented young people. Overhiring is the result, so overqualified employees end up doing routine, unexciting jobs until the invisible hand of competition eventually weeds them out. It is not pleasant to have a very real problem expressed in the form of a platitude.

A common promise, heard from almost every new expatriate executive taking over his company's Asian operations, is not very different from Pickle's own statement: 'Colour, creed, race, and religion have no place in our company. I promise I shall do everything in my power to see that an Asian will run this operation in the not-too-distant future.' Middle managers glance at each other, raise their eyebrows, and roll their eyes. They have heard it before; the memory haunts their egos and hurts their pride. Why do expatriates make these promises? The record should speak for itself.

The criteria for promotion

When people do get promoted, nobody is any the wiser about the criteria. Promotion announcements at the office daily come as a surprise and shock to a majority of employees. They wonder about the qualities needed to get ahead in the company. They don't know what their superiors consider important—is it loyalty, hard work, or seniority? Nor are they sure if breaking sales and profit records will get them ahead. They sense that vague factors quietly rule their fate—being liked by the boss, perhaps, or making slick presentations at company meetings. Others may think they need to be artful, devious, or downright dishonest to further their careers. How else can a person whom no one respects gain a position of power over them? Such feelings can harden into bitter cynicism, snapping morale, and belittling the value of honest hard work.

Nowadays most large companies use some system of performance evaluation to promote people. Still, not even their employees view all decisions as infallible or impartial. Though equipped with a general idea of the qualities sought in future leaders, employees may not be fully aware of their company's business plans: now aggressive growth, now cautious consolidation. Changed circumstances can make the promotion of different types of executives seem contradictory. Imagine, then, how much more mystified are those employees who are privy to neither performance criteria nor future plans. No wonder they become prey to confusion and disorder. They learn to jostle and jockey for advantage, to haggle and cheat for the next leg up.

It is unreasonable to expect the best from people who don't know what those exact expectations are. A factory assembler may be given a quota of ten widgets a day and his performance rated against that target, but the task of managers is longer-range than the immediate output of the day. They must know how to plan for business expansion while keeping a dedicated eye on the constant improvement of their operations. Since senior managers in multinationals get moved around frequently, they are unable to judge the long-range impact of these managerial qualities. They tend to appraise middle managers on traits and behaviour rather than on results. Therefore, employees can't be blamed for believing that the basis for promotion is biased and arbitrary.

The ultimate danger occurs when a person of little integrity lands the top job, causing the other employees to feel betrayed. Such a move gives recognition and prestige to values the employees could never admire. The new head of an Asian subsidiary of an international company, for instance, may be in the right place at the right time—but disaster is in store if it is not generally agreed amongst employees that he is the right man. Such decisions destroy the spirit of the local organisation and discredit the company. A high-level business appointment is a public as well as private act. It should be rational, not only from the point of view of business needs, but also on grounds of social and cultural acceptability.

A good performance appraisal system helps an organisation inspire its employees to achieve their best. It enables supervisors to sit down with their people from time to time, discuss how their efforts measure up to their tasks, and guide their career development. It also helps determine the size of salary increases. But no performance system is perfect. Some are obsessively devoted to the search for high-flyers, and serve to demoralise the bulk of 'solid citizens'. Nor are they entirely objective. Some companies use a multiple rating system in which several managers compare the performance records prepared by one supervisor with a number of other employees. This gratifies the egos of a lot of managers while shortchanging fairness. Also, because the employees see the appraisal process as closely linked to their salary increases, the system inhibits frank dialogue and becomes less satisfactory as a tool for personnel development. It reduces employees into categories of winners or losers. The most important point to remember is that each promotion announcement tacked on the notice board puts a firm's integrity on the line. A company reveals its nature by the type of people it promotes more than by anything else.

Career planning

Unfortunately, the task of developing people remains an ad hoc activity in most organisations. Even in companies which have a semblance of a system, it is a process which is subject to too many uncertainties. Anyone who has sat at a management development committee knows that it is like playing Monopoly. Though the senior executives look deadly serious, they are aware that the stakes are not real. As they flick through thick binders containing personal histories, performance appraisals, potential ratings, and proposed career paths of high-flying middle managers, they know they are playing God. But they also realise they have little control over how things will really turn out over the next five or ten years. In debating a divisional manager's qualifications as a future president of an affiliate, they recognise their judgments are only speculations at best. But they also know they have nothing to lose if he or she doesn't make it. Nor is the company worried because it can get another person for the job from a hundred other locations.

There is a very different dedication to advancing employee's careers in organisations which know they can ill-afford to waste talent in the search of candidates for succession to the top. Meeting someone like Rizalino Navarro, for instance, redeems one's faith in career planning. He was only 44 years old in 1982 when he stepped into the shoes of the founder, Washington SyCip, and became chairman of SGV & Co., the largest firm of chartered accountants in Southeast Asia. He had joined the company as a 20–year old junior auditor. Apart from a stint at Colgate-Palmolive and a leave of absence to take a Harvard MBA degree, Navarro has stuck with SGV and steadily climbed up its ladder: consultant (management services division), partner in the Thai affiliate, a return to Manila as partner and deputy head of management service, managing director (audit division), vice chairman, and finally chairman.

Localisation

International companies are under less pressure to develop Asian managers than Asian companies aspiring to become international. Foreign companies' reliance on home-country and other overseas locations to meet the needs of their Asian operations, especially new ventures, is almost as heavy as it was two to three decades ago. Recently two directors of a well-known American company sat in their suite at a Bangkok hotel sipping pre-lunch cocktails. In the next room, their legal and financial advisors were putting final touches on a proposal for a multi-million-dollar factory. Everyone was pleased with the concessions they knew they were going to extract from the Thai authorities. Twelve hundred kilometres away in Kuala Lumpur that same morning, the senior executives of a renowned Japanese manufacturing company were congratulating themselves on persuading the Malaysian government to provide ten hectares of prime industrial land for practically nothing. The satisfaction of the two companies was due to the low production costs they could now expect. But in their celebration neither party had given much thought to the crucial question of who would manage the operations. There was a cursory mention of specialists and start-up teams from the home office, but nothing about development of local management!

Despite all their talk about the 'pacific century' and their delight in the region's low labour costs, foreign investors are ignoring a vital factor that will return to haunt them—the widening gap between economic progress and the pace at which managers are being developed. Too many people vaguely assume that greater foreign investment will of itself lead to more trained managers. Hundreds of foreign companies in Asia are still managed by expatriates. Some of them have been here for a century or more. 'In most of these companies there are no senior local managers,' says Charas Xuto, former president of Siam Cement. He had begun his career with Esso Thailand and had risen to the ranks of middle management before moving to Siam Cement. 'Esso started its management development program 30 years ago but still it does not have a Thai general manager,' he adds. 'Even in Shell, it's the same thing. But Lever Bros. are good. They have a Thai chairman.'

Charas explains why he quit Esso:

> I worked for Esso for 18½ years. I like the way they develop people. After we changed from Standard Vacuum in the early '60s, the training program took over like a storm. I worked at the airport as a refuelling supervisor. We learned from the manual. Even later when I was in sales, there was a manual. These manuals were very good and also there were good teachers. Esso is a good training school. The reason I left was that there were not many prospects in Esso. I knew that I couldn't be a manager of Esso.

Was it a general perception of employees that a Thai national would not become general manager? 'Yes,' said Charas firmly. Had it been much more rewarding to join a national company? 'I have two kids. My plan was to send them abroad if I had enough money. So when I was offered better pay I took it. I felt that my experience in Esso would be useful in a national company. To be frank, I did not expect to become president of Siam Cement.' In the past, perhaps, it didn't matter a great deal, but these days can foreign companies afford to lose trained people when business is getting much more competitive? 'If they can stop that by providing higher opportunities, it would be good,' replies Charas. That's precisely what he accomplished in Siam Cement. He took the Esso program beyond the boundaries of middle management, liberating it from the constraints under which it had operated for over a quarter of a century:

> When I first joined Siam Cement, they had no development program at all for employees. So we had to set up a sort of training centre. In the old days they did not believe in the development of people. But now it has started working. During the time I was president, I emphasised training. I believe in the human asset. It is the most important asset. We have the policy to promote from within and in order to do that you have to develop your people. We developed across the board—junior supervisors, senior supervisors, and especially senior supervisors to become executives.

Charas stresses how this program differs from those with a narrower functional focus:

> One of the specific purposes of the program is to broaden the outlook of our managers. In the old days we were split into separate manufacturing and marketing companies and so on. Each looked after its own interests. We wanted our employees to see things as a whole, starting with production and on to marketing, finance, and supervision.

Every company which is a newcomer to the region starts its business believing it will be able to localise in due course. But without concerted plans and firm timetables, such commitments remain mere pious hopes. Most companies think it is simply a matter of grooming a handful of personnel. Since there is a tacit understanding that essential control will stay in the hands of executives from the head office, nobody gives priority to sustained programs for developing local managers. The American company mentioned above plans to import an entire production team from one of its plants in the USA and hasn't thought of hiring locally even a human resources manager. The Japanese company is no different. All its top positions will be filled by staff from other subsidiaries. The usual excuse is lack of suitably trained local personnel. But what are these companies doing to develop them? Hundreds of thousands of local managers will be needed if companies are to cope with economic expansion in the coming decades. Many firms are quick to cite on-the-job training, foreign assignments, rotational responsibilities, and other ways in which they identify and groom high-potential employees. But this is all done in the confined atmosphere of the corporation itself. There is little opportunity for employees to acquire the breadth of vision that will strengthen their claims to top positions. Occasionally managers may be asked to attend advanced management courses abroad. But the case histories they discuss and the hypothetical problems they solve invariably come from a different culture at a different stage of economic development. Much of what they learn is of academic value only.

A business education

Millions of dollars are spent every year by the same companies towards helping to fund management and business schools at home. The money from educational foundations set up by some of them is critical for programs devised by business schools to meet the needs of industry. No institution in Asia receives the kind of financial backing that is given to INSEAD in France or IMI in Switzerland. Without a top class business education, the Asian century will be a hollow dream. Correlli Barnett in his book *The Pride and the Fall: The Dream and Illusion of Britain as a Great Nation* cites the inadequately trained force of managers as one of the reasons for the decline of a once-proud country. Innovation was stifled, he says, by the so-called 'practical man'—the manager with little or no formal education and training who learned everything he knows on the job.

Meanwhile our existing management schools deserve greater attention than they have enjoyed so far. There is no reason why in due course their graduates should not enjoy a handsome premium over those returning from abroad. There is a lot to be said for a reversal of the old corporate policy of awarding preferred status to foreign degrees. The recognition is growing that techniques must be grounded in the context of the societies in which they are applied. Before the advent of management institutes in Asia, a young man with an MBA from a Western business school was automatically guaranteed a safe career. This is now changing as more and more companies realise that foreign training suppresses many of our cultural values that are critical to leadership and organisation-building in Asia.

Asian business schools are also becoming aware, albeit slowly, that there is less value in business courses borrowed from abroad than in developing their own programs tailor-made for local economic and social conditions. Gaston Ortigas, former dean of the Manila-based

Asian Institute of Management founded in 1968 says that AIM caters to Asian management needs by stressing four important things: entrepreneurship, cultural setting, agriculture and rural development, and government-business relations. AIM now boasts a total of over 14 500 alumni from more than 40 countries. Ortigas believes management education in Asia is in good shape, though enrolments need boosting. He told me that the Association of Deans of ASEAN Graduate Schools of Business, of which he was chairman when I met him in 1989, was putting the finishing touches on a joint PhD program. The association has fifteen members, four each from Indonesia, Thailand, and the Philippines, and one each from Malaysia, Singapore, and Hong Kong. Talking with Ortigas leaves one in little doubt that the time is not far off when managers and movers of the 'pacific century' will be increasingly equipped for the task in our own halls of learning. Says Tunku Iskandar, group managing director of Malaysia's Melawar Corp., and a 1979 graduate of the institute's Top Management Program, 'I found AIM helpful, as it put American business technology in an Asian context. That's important because the way we conduct business is different from how it is conducted in the West in some ways.'

Consciousness of local context is growing fast. Says Toemsakdi Krishnamra, director of Sasin in Thailand, 'We are not teaching enough about the Thai economy and Thai problems. So far we have produced only two courses: one on the Thai legal framework and the other on macroeconomics. We are also developing a course in cross-cultural management.' Toemsakdi expresses these sentiments despite the fact that Sasin which, from its inception in 1982 until 1987, was Chulalongkorn University's Graduate Institute of Business Administration, has been a remarkable success. He points out that a decade ago Thailand realised it had to get off the mark quickly to produce home-bred managers needed for the long-haul national development. 'So the program to establish the school was conceived with a goal to achieve quick results.' It was to be a cooperative endeavour between Chulalongkorn, Thailand's oldest and top-rated university and two leading business schools in the USA: Northwestern University's Kelogg Graduate School of Management in Chicago, and the Wharton School of the University of Pennsylvania.

However, professors fresh from the USA had to undergo thorough orientation. 'When the rector received the first group, he told them that Thais are very proud of their heritage,' says Toemsakdi. A tour was arranged of the country's venerable monuments. 'One professor was so enthused that when he had a chance he was instrumental in having the famous Vishnu lintel returned to us. He went to the Art Institute of Chicago and offered to raise funds to buy something to replace it.' The 1000–year old Khmer sandstone carving of the god

Vishnu reclining on a *naga* (semi-divine serpent) had once adorned a doorway of the majestic Phnom Rung temple in eastern Thailand. It vanished in 1960 and turned up thirteen years later in the Chicago Institute. It was returned to Thailand in 1988. In a way the story captures the spirit of Sasin: preserving the cultural past while preparing Thailand for a prosperous future.

Out of 24 faculty members, five are Thai and the rest from Kellog and Wharton. But the ratio may be more balanced in the future. 'We are thinking of inviting Columbia to join in. But even with three, we may not be able to man the expanded program and will need other professors from Asia.' Toemsakdi says, 'Education is an experiment. The challenge is whether we can train people as well in Thailand as by sending them abroad.'

Hong Kong Polytechnic's new Business and Technology Centre offers an integrated graduate development scheme modelled on the program run by Britain's University of Warwick. Its aim is to help managers in manufacturing to enhance their careers by way of a flexible, part-time curriculum at postgraduate level. Its 'systems' approach stresses the ways information can improve product lines from the factory to distribution. Computer-aided techniques play a crucial role, as does the significance of quality control. The course shows how to analyse problems and come up with creative answers using state-of-the-art production methods and strategies. It entails three years' study in twelve 'modules', each consisting of 40 hours of lectures, case studies, seminars, and home assignments. The Warwick staff takes part in teaching, and Hong Kong graduates receive the university's Master of Science degree in manufacturing systems engineering.

The 5000–member Malaysian Institute of Management is playing an important role in making management education available to a much wider spectrum of youth than in the past. Modern businesses in Asia have been traditionally managed by a small elite. Despite a handful of multi-millionaires of humble origins, most enterprises are run by a privileged establishment. One must come from a relatively rich family to afford the local university education, let alone a business degree. As these are *sine qua non* for entry into the magic circle, Asian managerial cadres are made up of people from society's upper strata. This has been particularly true of Malaysia. But MIM is being instrumental in democratising the executive ranks. Destined in the past to remain mere soldiers of commerce, young men and women of modest means can now look forward to becoming the captains of business and industry of the future. Manogaran Maniam, the institute's senior manager, says about its executive MBA program, 'It's our aim that it should be readily available to the average income-earner without his or her having to go and get a grant somewhere.

Ours is the least expensive program in the market.' The two-year program, during which students do weekend work, costs about US$300 a month. Under a cooperative arrangement, they earn an MBA degree from the University of Bath's School of Management, one of Britain's better-known business schools. While the program doubtless benefits from its overseas connection, Maniam is quick to stress that it is fully oriented towards Malaysia. 'The entire curriculum was devised and designed by Malaysians and is implemented by them,' he says. 'We did the whole thing. We did not buy over a program. We did not receive a franchise.' A colleague reinforces the point. 'It's not a transplant,' she insists, reflecting MIM's goal of evolving a distinctive Malaysian identity in management.

Yet management education, either from overseas or local schools, is no guarantee of success if one is unfortunate enough to pick a miserable company to work for. Contrary to your belief that your management prowess can conquer anything, you may find the challenge invincible. Fortified by barricades of incompetence, shielded behind layers of seniority, and ossified by an indifferent corporate culture, your new associates may pose an impregnable phalanx. That's reason enough for the Singapore Institute of Management, which celebrated its twenty-fifth anniversary in 1989, to emphasise a two-track approach: managerial development and organisational development.

Managers need skills to promote a company's fortunes, but companies must furnish the proper stage for using those skills. SIM offers to Singapore companies a variety of counsultancy services under a division headed by Ong Teong Wan. Essentially, he helps client firms answer three questions: Where are we right now? Where should we be heading? How do we get there? Sorting out this puzzle may entail introducing a mix of such methods as strategic planning, management by objectives, structural review, and operations-and-functions analysis. Often it also calls for rethinking the employee appraisal, compensation, and career development policies as well as coming to grips with the issues of leadership style and corporate environment.

A veteran personnel and training director for National Semiconductor and Union Carbide in Singapore, Ong realises the importance of adapting his knowledge to each situation. 'In my consultancy work, every organisation I work with is always a learning experience,' he says. 'I try to transfer the systems I learned with the multinationals to these companies, but within the local context. I change the systems around to suit the organisation.' How does one go about adapting the system of Management By Objectives (MBO)? Where teamwork is vital to the success of a business, Ong conducts a delicate grafting. Achieving results at the expense of a colleague becomes taboo. Performance appraisals reflect not only *what* an employee achieves but *how* he achieves it. 'If you transplant a foreign technique wholesale,' Ong says, 'you get tissue rejection.'

Is Asia limited forever to only adapting management ideas? Ong replies:

> We will certainly have our own concepts in certain things that we do. American systems, for instance, are very rational and formalised. I think there is a place in local businesses for *guanxi*: connections, face, long-standing trust, and understanding. The younger managers with MBA degrees are trained as technocrats. Those are useful systems but have to be placed in the context of business relations.

Why do some institutes put so much emphasis on producing inter-national managers when there is a crying need to groom truly Asian managers? Ong blames the influence of foreign teaching methods:

> We tend to lay a lot of stress on the intellectual and rational level—the thinking process in our management courses. There is a lot of room for training in the affective domain, where people across the table transmit a certain understanding and feeling for each other in order to do business. There is certainly room for being able to sense, for developing empathy. But most of our courses are cognitive. The greatest ones are all those quantitative courses that you see in MBA programs. There is a lot of room for more cross-cultural courses.

The independent approach

Meanwhile, attempts to transfer Western management skills to Asia fail every day. They are doomed because a simple fact is overlooked: people's minds are programmed differently by different life experiences. Behaviour patterns between supervisors and subordinates, among colleagues, and towards clients are established outside the work situation. They are conditioned by relationships between children and parents, students and teachers, and citizens and governments. Though there is nothing new about these facts, it was only in 1980 that they were substantiated by years of research among employees of a large multinational in 67 countries by Dr Geert Hofstede.

Hofstede's statistical analysis shows that differences among countries reflect the existence of four underlying value dimensions. First is the issue of individualism versus collectivism: preference for a loosely-knit social framework in which individuals take care of themselves, or for a tightly-knit system in which they expect their relatives to look after them. Second is the power distance: the extent to which members of a society accept the unequal distribution of power; this affects the behaviour of both the less and the more powerful. Third is the degree to which people feel uncomfortable with uncertainty and ambiguity. Societies that have a strong tendency to avoid uncertainty maintain rigid codes of belief and behaviour. They are intolerant towards deviant persons and ideas. The last value concerns social differentiation: preference for achievement, heroism, assertiveness, and material success on the one hand and relationship, modesty, caring for the weak, and quality of life on the other. Though accounting only for a small part of the differences in cultural systems, these four factors are important in understanding the functioning of organisations and the people within them. The assumption, for instance, that each individual is motivated by self-interest is untenable in a collectivist culture in which family or national interest may be considered paramount. Differences along the dimension of power will determine the need for subordinate consultation versus the acceptability of paternalistic management, affecting the style of leadership. 'Especially in the USA, ideas about leadership have often been developed into packages suitable for training and sometimes sold at a fee by consultants,' says Hofstede. 'These packages have been exported to other countries as magic recipes for management improvement.' He cites the example of MBO based on joint goal setting between superior and subordinate, assuming relative independence of the subordinate. But in societies that accord much higher power to the superiors, the subordinates will wait for a direct or indirect message to decide the objectives.

Hofstede has been challenged, however, by Tan Jing Hee, deputy executive director of SIM. Tan looks at the proposition differently. 'My view is that Western techniques like MBO have been found to work in the West, helping to improve the management of organisations and resulting in increased productivity and job satisfaction,' he says. 'It is therefore in our interest to consider whether they can be applied in an equally effective way here.' He adds that Hofstede's study indicates that Singapore's environment is unlike that of the West. It places a high value on the collective good, filial piety, and respectful loyalty to elders, including older senior managers and bosses. Consensus of opinion is preferred to confrontation. Hierarchical order is maintained by observance of rules and regulations. Is one therefore to conclude, asks Tan, that Singapore's cultural gap is too wide for an alien style like MBO? Tan suggests that Singapore organisations are likely to adopt a pragmatic approach, opening themselves to whatever management techniques are likely to work. 'At the same time there is some evidence that cultural characteristics are changing in Singapore,' he adds, 'especially along the individualism-collectivism dimensions.' He explains that in Hofstede's survey, Singapore was low on the individualism scale in 1970 as it was strongly correlated with its low GNP per capita. Since then it has become prosperous. 'If the strong correlations between individualism and GNP per capita hold true, then, as a society, we should be moving up the individualism scale,' he says. Obviously, he believes that this is now happening and, therefore, MBO should work in Singapore.

In a keynote speech at the 1989 International Management Development Network Assembly in Montreal, attended by over 175 deans from business schools throughout the world, Gabino Mendoza, who for almost ten years was president of the Asian Institute of Management, highlighted a temptation that has bedevilled the teachers of management education in the developing world:

> If you will fall down and adore Western management technology,
> teach your students its principles without questioning their premises,
> lecture them about its techniques without examining their applicability,
> prescribe to them its textbooks without scrutinising the underlying
> values that they espouse, you will become as all-knowing, as far-seeing,
> and as impeccable as a Harvard professor.

As one of the steps towards a more independent approach, Mendoza suggests a change in the source of management technology and teaching materials by greater reliance on local managerial communities rather than foreign academics. It is only through such interactive processes that Asian business schools will be able to evolve management systems that will more closely fit our societies' requirements, realities, culture, and aspirations, he recommends.

Meanwhile, management development at most multinational companies still stops at 40. A great many multinationals have an ingrained corporate prejudice and fear against mature Asian managers who are induced or forced to take early retirement. It is not difficult to identify the reasons for such an attitude. First, promotion prospects for Asians tend to be limited, so they stay in the job longer than expatriates. From the company's point of view this is not a bad thing. But often a young expatriate is put in charge of these experienced employees, making him or her feel uncomfortable. The second reason is purely economic: younger employees cost less. Thirdly, it's easy to promote a young employee every two or three years, and this helps reinforce the company's claim that its management development program is working. Older Asian employees are often an embarrassment because their presence is a constant reminder that the system works only up to a certain level. The fourth reason is a basic attitudinal difference: old age is frequently equated with obsolescence by Westerners, but accorded honour and deference by Asians. Whatever the reason, the tragic truth is that many companies fail to tap fully the rich experience of older Asian employees. It is no remedy to discard them simply because their experience outstrips the positions they hold. Forward-looking multinationals bypass the problem. They know these employees dedicate their working lives to the enhancement of corporate profits just as much as expatriates do—despite blocked careers, blunted aspirations, lower salaries, and missing stock options. Early retirement is a poor acknowledgement of their contribution and is a failure of management to recognise their worth.

My advice to Asian managers who work for insensitive multinationals is this: start in your mid-thirties or even earlier to plan a second career. Lay the groundwork before you have to deal with early retirement. You may be considered a hot-shot now, but make no mistake, you are already on a path of diminishing returns as far as your personal aspirations are concerned. Don't be fooled by a temporary foreign assignment or by leadership and supervision courses. They are not designed to help you reach the top. If you work for one of these companies, plan now to turn your training to your advantage. Most managers who have quit such places in time are faring much better in their second careers. Don't hang on in the hope of one day occupying the corner office. The criteria for promotion will be very different once you pass forty. Making a mid-career move may be the best thing you ever do.

7   Going global

We had just sat down to lunch in a Brussels restaurant when Maurice Mertens casually asked a question that left me speechless. He runs a small local advertising agency, and had been invited by a friend of mine, a manager with the European head office of an international company. Merten's agency had just been awarded the firm's Belgian business. I was amazed when he asked me how he should go about handling his new client's advertising in Asia from Brussels. Evidently he knew nothing of the highly competitive advertising business in this region. But—far more appalling, to my mind—he assumed that since he was now handling Belgian advertising for my friend's company, it would be natural for him to do the 'Asian side' too. Clearly, Mertens is a victim of 'globalisation'.

Almost every company that can afford a fax machine and an IDD facility talks of going global, and Asia is always seen as the great untapped opportunity. When a foreign-owned, Singapore-based firm opened a small office in Hong Kong recently, its founder proudly declared that it was just the beginning. Undeterred by his company's total revenues of less than $500 000 a year, he announced over champagne that Tokyo, Jakarta, and Sydney were next on his list. The gathering, which did not include a single potential customer, cheered loudly.

Mini-multinationals

In the case of small companies, this phenomenon can't really be called globalisation, which defines the international power and reach of megabuck corporations. Nor does it belong to the merger-and-acquisition trend, which entails a purchase of assets or share swap to create a single entity. It is a curious development that appears to be all of these things but in reality is none of them. Based on the flimsy premise that an apparent link with an outfit in Manchester improves your service to customers in Medan, the fad is to *look* global. For customers, unfortunately it is proving to offer the worst of all worlds. The trick is to make a company seem bigger than it is without using any cash—only a simple arrangement between an Asian company and a partner in North America or Europe. Each borrows part of the other's name and logo, makes a token exchange of directorships—and, hey presto, a multinational giant is born. To the Western company, the tie-up may give the feeling of venturing on the cheap into the 'pacific century'. But for the Asian partner it can mean an appalling transformation. Once entrepreneurial and customer-oriented, the company now clothes itself in the organisational hierarchy and trappings that have been discarded by even those who invented them. In short, it becomes a pitiful mini-multinational.

The customers, ostensible beneficiaries of this charade, find it utterly confounding. To ask about a new property development they ring a local estate agency. Formerly called 'Veritas', it is now known as 'Westminster Veritas International', no less. In the past they could get an earful from any of the salesmen. Now there is a separate department for everything. The company remains small, but it has built a daunting institutional edifice, transforming itself from a service company into a totally unresponsive outfit.

The same global urge is sending hordes of businessmen to Asia in search of a market for their gadgets, products, or innovations, many of which are still in the introductory phase in their own countries. Some are so new that they don't even qualify for the title of a passing fad. But that doesn't deter these latter-day Magellans from aiming for a slice of the Asian market. Their passion to sell, franchise, or manufacture their products here is based on a mixture of history and hope. The romantic memories of childhood stories of clipper ships carrying silk and spices are now rekindled by the daily emergence of a new NIC or Little Dragon. So they feel frustrated when they run into both business and bureaucratic obstacles. The zeal of these businessmen for globalisation is supported by the slogans of free trade. They cannot see why their product, the creation of an affluent post-industrial society, is not welcomed as the salvation of a developing economy. Frozen yoghurt, after all, is good for you. It is becoming part of the diet of thousands of health-conscious Californians. So why should it not sell in a supermarket in Sikkim? If you think that's far-fetched, consider the following front-page story that appeared in a regional business publication: under a headline blazoning the message to the world that foreign investors are turning sour in Korea, a correspondent based in Seoul cites the case of an investor who has been held up for six months by the government over his request to import American cracker crumbs for his cheesecake ice cream. This is offered seriously as an example typifying red tape and a selective (read: discriminatory) approach to foreign investment.

To be fair, the same story quotes a businessman who explains that Koreans want foreign investment in high-tech fields where they need it but are not so excited about low-tech projects. But this apparently does not satisfy the global ideologists who are aghast at every instance of delay or doubt.

In the post-colonial era many developing nations were haunted by the spectre of foreign control of their economies. They devoted the bulk of their resources to import substitution. As they became increasingly self-reliant, they started pulling down some of the old barriers to foreign investment and free trade. One should encourage this process. Advanced technology in telecommunications, durable consumer goods, transport, modern banking, and computer industries, to name just a few, can bring huge benefits to developing countries. These needs are global, and international companies have an important role to play in satisfying them. Unfortunately, for every serious investor there are ten peddling products whose only relevance is to a lifestyle of abundance and wasteful disposability. Their whimsical ventures subject the idea of positive globalisation to ridicule. People deprived of necessities may feel cheated when they see money flowing into the creation of luxury goods.

One-sidedness

Globalisation is overwhelmingly one-sided: extension of American and European companies to the rest of the world. With the exception of Japanese companies, there are few Asian multinationals with a global reach similar to that of the Western giants. Against this historical tradition, even those who are expanding outside their national borders are doing so in almost tip-toe fashion. My discussion with Alan Yeo, chairman of Yeo Hiap Seng, Southeast Asia's leading food and beverage company, illustrates the point. Despite a $52 million acquisition in the USA, one of the largest ever by a Singapore company, he talks of expansion along a familiar, cautious route. With government-owned Temasek Holdings as a silent partner, YHS purchased Chun King, the second-largest producer of pre-packaged East-Asian foods in the USA, from RJR Nabisco. Its strategy is to expand sales to Asians abroad. 'It's a realistic plan, being able to sell to people you know, people of the same origin,' he says. 'I don't think any Singaporean company or other companies from Asia could march into the UK and expect to produce a typical British product—Batchelors or Beecham—or go to the USA and try to be General Foods.' Yeo is gratified that the one-man cottage industry his father founded in the 1930s to produce soy sauce has grown to meet so many wider needs of Asians who have gone abroad to settle or study.

'If that's successful,' he reflects, 'then the Caucasians and supermarkets are more likely to stock our products. To go to a supermarket chain in any part of the world is difficult. They are interested in volume turnover. In our minds we have to scale it all back to Singapore and the size of the company. In the world we are just a drop.'

The same hesitancy—or 'realism'—is reflected in the company's expansion to other parts of Asia. Any Asian food company, Yeo feels, would find it hard to become a strong continent-wide presence, partly because of many protectionist regimes. Those that do succeed in crossing borders, he notes, tend to follow patterns of migration and blood ties. It is obvious that the historical experience still acts as a constraint to the future growth plans of Asian companies. But Western multinationals take it for granted that the world is their market. They are not deterred by protectionist regulations from entering into profitable joint ventures. Asians find it hard to compete with companies which are already global. 'I won't go to the USA to produce a cola to compete with Coke or Pepsi,' says Yeo. 'I don't think there is any point in banging one's head against a stone wall and hoping the wall will break.'

Conformity

The same diffidence affects Asian managers in their career aspirations with global companies. They know that it would be like banging their heads against a stone wall to expect managerial positions beyond a certain level in a global organisation. Their advancement does not depend on other senior Asian colleagues because there are very few of them around. They must carry a stamp of approval from a Western boss to get along in a global company.

Boon Yoon Chiang, chairman of Jardine Matheson Holdings (Singapore) Ltd joined the company 22 years ago as its public relations manager. Today he is one of the three Asian directors of the 17–member regional board of Jardines, a Hong Kong blue chip whose business has traditionally concentrated on the Asia-Pacific theatre. Looking back, he considers his experience overseas with Jardines, especially a 1974–75 stint in the Hong Kong head office, as most important to his career. How did he react to the colonial culture of the company in those days? 'The fact that I am a Singaporean possibly makes it easier for me to mix with expatriates,' he explains. 'Also, I was asked to go there for a specific reason. I think people treated me in a different way, perhaps.' Singaporeans, he believes mingle with expatriate colleagues more freely. 'In Hong Kong they don't do that, partly because people at home and outside the workplace speak Cantonese. That might be a reason. But that is not true in Singapore.' Then he adds, with a sense of realism, 'Of course, Hong Kong is still a colony, whether you like it not.'

Boon finds his expatriate colleagues very understanding. 'They treat me as if I am one of the key staff in the organisation. Maybe I am fortunate that all along over the years I have worked for European expatriate bosses, or bosses of bosses in Singapore.' Is it possible that he now looks at things through rose-tinted glasses as distinct from the view of others who have not reached the top? He mentions the wind of change in today's executive ranks: 'Even ten years ago people never thought that we would have a Singaporean running Jardines in Singapore. Fifteen years ago nobody dreamed a Singaporean would be running IBM in Singapore.' A realist, who knew how to bide his time until the right moment, Boon was elected chairman of the Singapore International Chamber of Commerce in 1987, the first Singaporean to hold the position in its 151–year history. Why did it take the chamber (a body whose name would suggest that it ardently believes in globalisation) so long to elect a local chairman? 'It's a very difficult question to answer,' says Boon hesitatingly.

When promotion does come, it may bring problems that are still associated with the old mentality. The qualities that foreign corporations expect in a promotion-worthy Asian often clash with virtues that are honoured in the Asian's own culture. This sense of disorientation can make high positions unbearable for Asian executives. Two years ago, Victor Goh became the first Singaporean to head the local office of a multinational company with over 20 years' experience there. Victor has been with the company since day one and has worked in both its regional and worldwide headquarters. But he is bitter because he feels his company has failed to show him more confidence and support. The company had assigned his predecessor without once asking whether he would get on with the staff; it was taken for granted that others would have to get on with him. 'In my case they asked a thousand questions, to the point that it became a public debate. This has undermined my authority. It's as if the company were waiting for me to fail.' Victor also blames visiting executives who show less cordiality to him than to his forerunner. 'It's entirely social and cultural, but others notice it.' He cites the recent visit of a vice-president and his wife. They contacted the family of an expatriate with another company, some friends of friends, to shop and socialise with. An invitation by Victor and his wife was politely turned down.

Often the pressure to imitate a foreign management style which is inconsistent with local social norms creates an unpleasant dichotomy in the minds of Asian managers in a global outfit. In Japan, after years of in-house clamouring, a foreign company finally appointed a

Japanese vice-president. If Kato did well, it was widely believed, he would replace the expatriate president. But things did not go well. Work at the USA head office had sadly given him a split personality in management styles. He often lost his temper and once chastised an old employee for his poor written English in front of scores of colleagues. People did not know where they stood with him, and in the end he was transferred.

Materially, a large corporation may provide a more rewarding career and better work environment. But its influence and control over its managers is more pervasive than ever—despite the so-called age of the individual and repeated assertions that institutions are trying to adapt to the shift. I recently met my old friend Jim, whom I had not seen for two years. I first met him about twelve years ago just after he had been transferred from Melbourne to the Asia-Pacific regional office of his huge company. Because of his marketing background, he stood out among his colleagues, most of whom were engineers. He felt protected by a special aura even though his conduct was considered unusual in a company that thrived on conformity. But Jim was to discover that his image was a liability. Behaviour tolerated at first as a mark of individuality was later condemned as failure. He was passed over for promotion. Though still considered a good marketing man, he did not fit in with the company's idea of a good manager. The more he was pressured to conform the more he rebelled. He tried in vain to dent the basic corporate culture, which was overwhelmingly oriented towards manufacturing. He came to understand that the match was unequal. It was about this time that Jim began destroying his own career. He took more latitude at work. He went out for extended lunches. His smoking and drinking became excessive. He was demoted and sent back to Melbourne. The company, he sighed, had destroyed his life:

> At every step they tried to make me a clone of other managers.
> I resented the manipulation. I offered them my professional
> expertise, but was not prepared to compromise my integrity as an
> individual...they adopted me then destroyed me; they didn't tell me
> I was supposed to embrace their computerised version of a manager.
> They had no idea how to harness individual talent. They were good at
> nurturing infants but did not know how to handle adults.

Jim's global company had never learned to value individual contributions. They hired him to inject a new marketing dimension into the company, but never understood the pressure on him to adapt to a monolithic organisation.

Superficially, a global concept is emerging, but in reality national differences are becoming more accentuated. Understanding other cultures is exacerbated in a multinational company by the pursuit of a common business aim and an overlay of company values and behaviour. Sir John Harvey-Jones, former chairman of Imperial Chemical Industries, says in his book *Making it Happen: Reflections on Leadership* that the true international company does not exist yet; and that that day won't come until representatives of overseas operations sit on the main board. 'We need a much greater sensitivity to the habits, values, and mores of other countries.'

Management, Sir John adds, is more of an art than a science. A manager must constantly improve the palette, colour, and skills of application of his art, which ultimately lies in helping people to do their best. Power used through a hierarchical organisation or the force of one person's determination will always be defeated by free men working in concert, under enabling leadership. Individuals everywhere are refusing to be codified, grouped, or collectivised. Unless companies change, they won't attract the best—and so will die. 'I pride myself on retaining my values as an individual while working for my company. I honour my company for its willingness to accept me and my idiosyncracies,' Sir John adds. Members of one's firm should be treated like family. 'People may think that in a rigorous competitive situation there is no room for the caring company... It is unfortunate that so many confuse caring, involvement, and compassion with out-dated concepts of paternalism.'

Joint ventures

Most multinationals are still run as if they were American or European companies. The emerging trend towards joint ventures often throws up conflicts where overseas partners are treated with distrust and dislike. Bill Hoffman, now a successful property developer in the USA, recalls his years of hard labour for one such giant. What stands out in his memory is the day he had to present a proposal to the board for a joint venture in Japan. He had put in six months' hard work on the project, which had been blessed by almost every executive in any way connected with the company's business in Asia. 'I had hardly put the first graph on the machine,' he says, 'when the chairman groaned, "All we need is another can of worms in Japan!"' Hoffman has only a hazy recollection of how the project got approval after such an inauspicious start.

Jaye Shagun remembers the time he asked about joint ventures at a meeting during a visit by Westbig's president. In front of managers from all over Asia, this dignitary snapped, 'I absolutely abhor joint ventures. I hate the very idea!' He did not explain how the company planned to grow when, as competitors were making clear, joint ventures stood to be the only way in the industry to retain market share.

Over the years, the Japanese undertaking which Hoffman helped launch has blossomed into the most successful project his old company has anywhere. It has chalked up records for quality, energy efficiency, productivity, and safety. It is held up as a model to the company's manufacturing operations across the world. Westbig, now under a new president and facing competition from several new quarters, has also been forced to adapt its ways. Technology is no longer as scarce as it used to be. Nor are the relative newcomers to Asia so fussy about absolute control. Indeed, they find local partners a positive asset.

But dinosaurs slow to evolve out of the age of oligopoly have missed many choice opportunities. Now some are even clamouring to sell their old technology in the open market—to few takers. However, in products where a couple of companies have carved up the global market amongst themselves, they guard the technology like corporate jewels. This helps them keep prices up. Despite repeated approaches by at least two developing countries for joint ventures to manufacture specialty synthetic rubber, the two world giants have turned up their noses at them. That certainly does not support the global club's claim of helping to transfer technology to developing countries. Thus, even though companies recognise how useful joint ventures can be in today's dramatically more competitive Asian arena, old prejudices still persist. The main reason, masked by many pretentious excuses, has often been the ignorance or arrogance of a single VIP. The chairman who had called the Japan strategy a can of worms was ethnocentric and had never worked abroad. To him, anything was inferior if it was not the form of management he knew. The Westbig seigneur who volubly disdained joint ventures was simply exhibiting his intolerance of the idea of sharing his absolute authority. Ten thousand shareholders are no problem, but a joint venture partner can seem to pose a real threat to one's power.

The usual areas of possible conflict such as respective duties and functions of partners, allocation of costs and profits, and protection and transfer of technology are not the areas that normally sour a relationship. Agreements spell these out clearly to avoid such pitfalls. Often the problem is the unwillingness to manage by consensus or to harmonise visions. For Asian managers who work with multinationals, nothing is more painful than cavalier head office treatment of partners who are highly respected in their own communities. Most joint ventures founder not on practical considerations but on that old devil pride. The bigger the company, the greater the pride of its top executives.

Asian-style management

In its worst form, globalisation demands that people give up their national identities. In management, this leads to the creation of giant business organisations whose subsidiaries spread out over the world are centrally controlled from a head'office thousands of miles away. It promotes styles of business and people development that are rooted in the home culture of the global organisation. It provides the senior executives of large companies the rationale to recreate the world in their own image, making overseas managers feel outsiders. It breeds intolerance for any other style of management except the one practised at the head office.

Globalisation deprives us of the chance to nurture a management style that would stress the qualities needed to cope with future business growth in Asia. These qualities could be summed up under the title SEEK—service, ethics, entrepreneurship, and know-how. Service to the customer, community, and country will be the hallmark of really successful companies. They and their products must be seen as improving life. The rewards reaped in profit will match the social value they add to their products. In any long economic downturn, products of marginal value will simply disappear. Companies constantly repositioning themselves as 'up-market' will fare far worse than those that have established themselves as suppliers of worthwhile things at a reasonable cost. In Asia, well-known family-owned businesses enjoy a high degree of customer loyalty because of a reputation for good value for money. This trust is a precious asset. As old operations grow into large public companies, new professional managers must try to preserve the old values that fostered it.

Ethics will be a critical factor. More than simply observing laws, paying taxes, and abjuring graft, it will include fair treatment of people. Autocratic businesses will attract low-quality employees. Firms with a name for treating individuals on merit, for providing training and opportunity, will prosper. Entrepreneurship will be a key requirement in an environment of rapid economic development, increasing competition and frequent business cycles. While maintaining a core business, companies will have to explore the potential of newer products. Investment opportunities abroad will demand a willingness to take risks. But purely speculative investments in property and the like will not be seen as any mark of entrepreneurship by the host nations, which will expect foreign investors to pioneer new industries.

Know-how in technical matters will be highly emphasised. While joint ventures with foreign partners will still be important, leading Asian companies will develop a know-how appropriate to local economic needs. Domestic research and development will help overcome barriers of quality and customer acceptance. Foreign brands will no longer enjoy an automatic high price differential. Closer economic cohesion in North America and Europe will stimulate reactions in Asia in favour of regional goods. There will be much more sharing of know-how, with Korea, Hong Kong, Taiwan, and Singapore investing in other South and Southeast Asian countries. Japan's investment in the region will increase dramatically.

Asian businessmen are often criticised for lacking these four qualities of service, ethics, entrepreneurship, and know-how— paradoxically the very ones that derive from old Asian values. Though undermined by globalism, service was the tenet on which old businesses were founded. Ethics and entrepreneurship were essential traits of businessmen in an era when large transactions were sealed by a man's word. The traditional emphasis on know-how and dedication to perfection is amply reflected in the old arts, handicrafts, and architecture, and has to be restored in this machine age. Without such underpinnings, borrowed management techniques will never give us pride in ourselves.

The one-market myth

The global gurus love to look at the world as a single market. The availability of Coke or Pepsi in most Asian cities, however, does not prove that the world has uniform tastes, habits, and needs. It's strange that we should need frequent reminders of this simple fact. Examples are cited daily in the business press of such successes as achieved by Johnson & Johnson in Japan by adapting its 'Reach' toothbrush to the local market or the popularity of Nippon Lever Corporation which acts as an essentially Japanese company belonging to the Unilever group rather than just a corporate manifestation of Lever in Japan.

The fashionable myth of global markets is one of the greatest problems of moving products into new cultural environments, according to George Fields, author of the book *From Bonzai to Levis*. 'I don't agree at all with the principle that all members of the world's middle class are exactly the same and therefore consume the same products,' he argues. 'The fact that many Japanese people now eat McDonalds's hamburgers and Kentucky Fried Chicken has absolutely nothing to do with their values. Few people who come to market their goods in Japan realise that the market for those same products is very different here and, if consumer motivation is studied, Japanese values are completely different.' Fields emphasises that Westernisation and modernisation are entirely different. 'It so happens that modern products have originated in the West since the industrial revolution, so that when we see a non-Westerner consuming modern products we think he's becoming "one of us". It's the Africans and Coca-Cola syndrome all over again.'

The one-market approach can be even more damaging to the developing countries when used to justify sites for large industrial plants. It is argued, for instance, that because it is more economical to build a world-scale 500 000–ton steam cracker to make ethylene, it should be located in the USA or Europe where there is much bigger demand for this basic chemical, which is used in the production of raw materials for plastics. It is suggested that since the demand in Malaysia, Thailand, or the Philippines each calls for only 100 000–ton capacity, these countries should import raw materials for their plastics industries. Overcapacity abroad is publicised to warn developing nations that if they build their own plants they would be adding to the glut in the world market—thus making it difficult for potential investors to raise money. The developing countries should wait, the argument goes, until they reach a stage when they can justify world-scale plants. It is not explained how these countries would ever reach that stage if they forego building local manufacturing capacity in industries vital to their economic growth. Nor is it mentioned who is responsible for creating overcapacity. Meanwhile, when there is a shortage of a product, Asian plastics factories are held hostage to high prices. No wonder global companies hate the idea of appropriate technology, let alone the concept of 'small is beautiful'.

Due to an explosion in the information available, business publications are particularly prone to the global market syndrome. But they don't often realise its inherent complexities. In an interview with *Media* some years ago, Peter Kann, founder editor of the *Asian Wall Street Journal*, said, 'We thought we could just transfer news from the *Wall Street Journal* into Asia and then by having Asian news staff—four reporters and four copy editors—we could give the paper an almost Asian content—like frosting on the cake.' But, he added, 'That was a fundamental mistake.' Eventually the staff was boosted significantly. 'Other publishers feel that their role is to bring news into Asia and dump this on people,' said Kann. 'We are a different publication. Our fundamental role is, of Asia for Asia.'

Global management

Despite the visible trappings of position and power, expatriate managers in charge of Asian operations of global corporations have little influence with their head offices. A senior manager told me of the key discussions that took place at the New York head office of his company to review some important policy. He hadn't been invited to participate because he wasn't considered senior management. Even though the operation he runs in Asia is big and profitable, it is not very significant in relation to the business his company does in the USA and Europe. But he was later expected to implement the policy in Asia without ever having had the opportunity to express his views. No wonder these representatives are considered ineffective leaders by the Asian managers who work with them. They perceive them merely as coordinators who spend much of their time reporting to head office. Matsuoka Toshio of the corporate planning office of Matsushita reinforces that view. 'It seems that foreign managers are very good at pointing out to headquarters what's wrong with the Japanese system. They readily express their ideas even to congress-men,' he says. When foreign executives are assigned as heads of Tokyo offices, he has noticed that 'the first thing they do is search for a beautiful office in a beautiful building. Then they look for a gorgeous apartment. After that, they start busily reporting to their head offices.' Lack of authority inevitably leads to lack of vision. One can recount scores of examples of expatriate managers who lack the courage to accept leadership in personnel policies, marketing strate-gies, pricing, and manufacturing investments. They are terrified that a local action may be considered inconsistent with global policies.

Asians, of course, have a better understanding of the local situa-tion, and can help in developing well-argued cases for modification to policy to suit local needs. But since they are even further down the corporate ladder, they have little say. A multinational which sum-moned executives from around the world to discuss future invest-ments in areas of potential growth did not invite a single Asian or Australian manager because none ranked highly enough. The expatriate manager who represented Asia–Pacific did return with an approved reassurance about the importance placed on the region. Predictably, the statement lacked credibility among employees.

Many large international companies will be hard pressed to come up with the name of a single product which they have developed directly in response to the needs of Asian customers. For so long they have looked upon Asia as a market for 'opportunistic sales'. Their tendency has been to promote the identical product everywhere, even if it is over-designed for local needs. It was left to a Japanese produc-er of fork-lift trucks, for instance, to find out that over 80 per cent of the market had reduced product-performance requirements which could be met at a 20 per cent cost saving. Since the customers of multinationals are in Asia and the factories overseas, there is very little coordination between marketing and manufacturing. When the product fails the Asian customer is blamed for using it improperly.

Even management fads are introduced globally. A few years ago many large corporations launched worldwide campaigns on the need to get close to the customer. That was considered the 'in thing' at the time. It heralded the dawn of a new awareness, a blinding realisation that customer satisfaction is the most critical factor in the success of a business. How did these companies forget it so soon? It's because their managements had embraced the concept only as a convenient excuse for altering policies, not as an article of faith. In the name of the customer, they changed and chopped their organisations and cut staff rather than enlarge their markets. Didn't Peters and Waterman, the authors of *In Search of Excellence* say that 'American companies are being stymied not only by their staffs, but also by their structures and systems, both of which inhibit action.' Leaner organisations were supposed to excel in customer service—but soon after decimating their workforces, the companies went back to their old ways.

Almost twenty years ago a giant international company invited the views of opinion leaders in eight Asian countries on foreign business in their countries. Three main criticisms emerged. First, foreign investors did not recognise the needs and aspirations of their host countries. They didn't bother to try to understand the problems and motivations of the people with whom they worked. They were interested only in exploiting the market or resources of the host country, giving only lip service to helping with economic development. Second, foreign companies did not promote their national employees to positions of real authority. Showcase nationals, with titles but no real responsibilities, had proved to be sad experiences for both parties. The companies discriminated against local employees in terms of salaries. Third, foreign investors ignored the need for more local participation or multinational ownership of international companies. They operated through wholly-owned subsidiaries and did not publish annual results which were 'consolidated' in their global reports. This practice gave rise to accusations that profits of foreign investors were too high and often resulted from unethical practices. It was also felt that disclosures by foreign firms to government and public were not open and complete, and that local reinvestment of profits was too low.

Have these companies changed in the last twenty years? Are those criticisms no longer valid? Some progress has no doubt been made. But many companies remain essentially the same, attracting mostly the same negative reactions. What makes matters worse is that under the new wave of globalisation, these companies now don't even feel the need to invite Asian views. The chief executive of the same company which had conducted the survey summed up the situation recently, 'I think we are uniquely international,' he told a Japanese trade journal during a visit. 'Something over one-third of our business is in the USA, a little over one-third is in Europe and Africa, and the rest is in the Asian–Pacific area, Latin America, and Canada. We like that, and intend to keep it that way.' He was obviously referring to the company's geographical spread. It didn't even occur to him that the reporter had asked him whether he thought his company was international in the context of multicultural partnership which the opinion leaders had highlighted two decades ago.

Globalisation of business will be a perilous thing if it is not accompanied by a greater measure of international understanding. In 1988, Keidanren (Japan Federation of Economic Organisations), created a committee for the promotion of inter-cultural understanding. Nishio Shin-ichi, chairman of the committee and of the Dai-Ichi Mutual Life Insurance Co. board, explained:

> The committee represents an attempt to obtain first-hand information on the diverse needs and interests of foreign countries and respond to such needs as far as possible at a time of the globalisation of corporate activity. It is my feeling that the world is entering a new age in which corporate activities and cultures are closely linked and in which private business plays a positive role in promoting inter-cultural understanding.

One of the first steps in such an understanding should be to realise what globalisation means to people in different countries. When Joy Jakobovitz, a 1988 graduate of Kalani High School, Honolulu, tells a local newspaper she wants to go into the field of international business, she visualises herself as an executive with a large American multinational; she thinks of travelling and an expatriate position abroad. But to Nirmala, in Kuala Lumpur, who graduated from school the same year and now works as a teller with a British bank, globalisation is an abstraction.

Globalisation enhances opportunities for employees working with the Western units of multinationals, often at the cost of Asian employees. When Westbig corporation abolished its Asia-Pacific office, it simultaneously expanded its regional set-up in Europe. Its Asian units now report to Brussels. The Asian spirit that took years to build is all but destroyed. Gone also are some of its best managers. Its regional office offered a unique opportunity to middle managers for higher positions. They enjoyed a broad responsibility in dealing with people and business on a regional scale. But now Westbig has transferred senior jobs, and prospects for them, out of Asia.

None of the original reasons for the establishment of the regional office twenty years ago have disappeared. Among the incentives was that of tapping into the Asian market's growth and profit potential. Though selling things produced elsewhere was lucrative, a sounder long-term strategy demanded some manufacturing within Asia. Investigators scouting for opportunities—specialists in market research, project studies, and supply-and-demand planning—needed a regional base. In line with this, Westbig also sought to help its Asian affiliates grow by providing them with a pool of expertise close at hand. Another reason was the need to put in place a senior team dedicated to building bridges to high Asian officials. Besides assessing how established laws stood to affect business, these corporate ambassadors were fielded out to gain a voice in future government policies. More generally, the regional office aimed to demonstrate to customers, employees, and opinion leaders, a strong commitment to Asia. All these things are still needed. But the wave of globalisation has made it easy to dispense with any notions of decentralisation, delegation, local autonomy, or multicultural management.

8   The corporate culture of stonecutters

There are offices that instantly fill you with bad vibes as soon as you walk through the door: black marble walls and Roman pillars, for example, make you wonder whether you are in the foyer of a turkish bath. On the surface such premises are examples of poor office design, yet they also reflect a more serious problem: lack of a clear idea of the distinctive features of their organisation on the part of management. The way their offices are designed is a minor, though obvious, aspect of their ill-defined corporate culture. In its more serious forms this vagueness can affect everything: corporate communications, customer service, the dispensation of power, the treatment of employees, the concept of mutual loyalty, the organisational structure, productivity, and planning. The underlying basic beliefs and values of a company determine its behaviour and the way it conducts its business. One company, for instance, may be authoritarian and, therefore, practice a totally top-down approach in its communication with employees. Another may depend on consensus and thus rely on multi-directional communication. These values are pervasive and deeply ingrained. They are common throughout the organisation and are followed by employees habitually and spontaneously. Most importantly, they are built up over years, not ordained overnight.

Unfortunately, in recent years we have been subjected to a series of quick-fix methods to create a new company culture. Your company has a history of bad employee relations? Well, a consultant will advise, just discuss things more often with employees and that should help clear the air. Employees don't have the incentive to improve quality? Okay, introduce an award to help make the culture more innovative. What makes such superficial measures even more futile is that they are implemented by the same managers who have lost the trust of their people. After a decade of cutting staff, penny-pinching, and raising of their own salaries, senior managers steeped in a conviction of their own superiority now believe that they can change corporate culture by a few shibboleths or sermons. They introduce gimmicks to evade real problems. They seek immortality through the use of ephemeral ideas, and expect transformation through acronyms and clichés. But these are mere distractions and do more harm than good. From the point of view of the Asian manager, they are aimed only at the symptoms, and do not address what truly ails the corporate body.

Unworthy of loyalty

Morita Akio of Sony calls a company a fate-sharing body. He describes the shared feelings that animate the Japanese firm as a 'sense of mission, a sense of participation, and a sense of achievement.' Mutual loyalty is the cornerstone of success. Confusion arises when some multinational companies expect and demand this degree of loyalty from their employees. Any team of top brass, however, that sets out to introduce massive reorganisation should be aware that employee loyalty will be one of the first casualties. A series of events in the past decade has dramatically changed attitudes among the bulk of employees. Illegal and unethical practices, environmental disasters, the neglect of safety, and corporate restructuring have all but decimated the concept of loyalty. Most Asian managers instinctively want to be loyal. They long for an employer worthy of their faith. They want to belong to and help advance an enterprise in whose values they can believe. But a company that poisons people, pollutes seas, kills workers, and takes pride in scaring its employees is not worthy of loyalty.

An arrogant management forfeits its claim to employee commitment. The head of a large company recently stated that he was thrilled that his employees no longer sleep well. Another boastfully described how he had ordered the closure of a whole division without hearing a squeak. In such a climate, managers feel professionally threatened. When an unhappy employee resigns, it is presented as a welcome case of 'good riddance'. Management would have everyone believe that the departing employee's performance was below par, that he was disgruntled, and that an opportunity is at hand to fill the slot with someone more level-headed and dynamic. Of course, nobody suggests that something might be wrong with the company's corporate culture. The top brass is rarely willing to concede that it may be out of touch with the workforce. The boss is always supposed to be well informed. A comforting belief, but as a rule it's a misconception that comes back to haunt the company when things become unstuck and morale takes a dive.

Many companies believe they treat their people better than do most

other employers. Comparative surveys or studies are deemed un-
necessary. The ruling powers are simply convinced that their minions
receive more than fair treatment. Many a corporate high command
cherishes the myth that their oufit is unique. Even in cyclical industries they remain confident that their company will be able to cope
with the next downturn. When the crunch comes, their lie hits them
smack in the face. They are then too busy picking up the pieces,
slashing budgets, laying off people and closing factories to offer a
word of explanation to the bewildered employees.

Language of connivance

One sees the gulf between image and reality, words and deeds, every
day in corporate pronouncements and publicity. Cigarette manufac-
turers would have us think that nothing other than community spirit
leads them to sponsor sports. Chemical companies want everyone to
know that they are the saviours of our environment. Everything they
issue about themselves is accompanied by photographs of happy
children climbing trees or sheep grazing in green meadows in the
shadow of smokestacks. One of their 'core values', they tell the
world, is to give Mother Nature a helping hand.

Employees in such companies learn to bend the rules and call it
experience. They compromise their personal integrity and blame it on
the 'real world'. They begin to sheath their conscience in corporate
clichés. Yet there are people who ask blunt questions that penetrate
the corrosive layers of self-deception. My friend, Jambon, is one such
person. Tony Trip had just finished his presentation on 'manpower
optimisation' when Jambon asked thoughtfully, 'How many people
are going to be fired?' Trip was the human resources manager of
Westbig Corporation. He looked at Jeremy Pickle, the president for
Asia-Pacific. 'I think you've missed the point,' said Pickle. 'We're
not talking about firing anyone. This exercise may reveal that we
actually need more people.' In their hearts everyone knew Jambon
had asked the pertinent question, but they kept quiet.

On another occasion the discussion concerned a manufacturing
project. Westbig's environmental conservation coordinator took the
lead in outlining the concept of 'acceptable risk'. The effluent,
he explained, would be chemically treated and the solid toxic waste
buried deeply some distance from the plant. 'We're within the
threshold. I know we're dealing with poisonous stuff, but there's no
immediate danger. And remember, there's no such thing as zero risk.'
Jambon, as usual, asked the apparently naive question: 'Is it possible
that in years to come the toxic wastes could seep into the under-
ground water supply?' The conservation coordinator smiled benignly

at the artless enquiry. 'Yes, it's possible, but by that time we'll all be dead.' Everybody laughed and the meeting was adjourned.

Jambon is unable, in such cases, to reconcile the reality with the niceties of corporate language. He once remarked that the company's 'strategic planning' project meant that it was going to get out of certain markets. Again, when Westbig was going through a cost-cutting exercise, something it did from time to time, it sent Jambon's supervisor to a meeting in Nice, France, of managers from around the world, to discuss the company's new 'cost-consciousness campaign'. Jambon thought the Riviera, playground of the rich, hardly the most conducive spot to explore new ideas on reducing expenses.

Surviving by cynicism

Other managers like Kenneth Kwan learn to survive through sheer cynicism. 'Listen to this,' he exclaimed as he joined our small group the other evening. 'The meeting is just over. It was Choh's turn to be interviewed. Management says it's serious this time about finding out what's wrong with customer service. Trust old Choh to do the number on them.' Kenneth laughed as he described how Choh had enthralled the visiting vice president with his tales of satisfied customers. No problem with prices or quality; they were willing to pay a bit more to maintain good business relations; they were patient about quality, being confident it would eventually be set straight. 'You see, three months ago another fellow had come, and it was Fred's turn,' Kenneth explained. 'Fred painted a rosy picture of our standing with customers and praised his boss to the skies for teaching him everything he knew. Two weeks later he was promoted over Choh who had criticised the treatment of our smaller customers.'

The trouble with people, said Kenneth, is that they don't realise the Asian operations of most large companies are still run the way they were 50 years ago: they are wholly owned branches; they don't publish annual reports; they have no local shareholders. Kenneth recalled a press luncheon at which a visiting director had rhapsodised about tremendous sales growth in Asia. Then a reporter asked about earnings. The company did not believe in disclosing that figure for the region, the director had said. Kenneth smiled broadly: 'That tells you that you are a fool if you believe that your Asian operations have their own identity. Your job is to sell to, not satisfy, customers, and least of all inform the public what you are up to!'

At this stage we were joined by Larry, an expatriate colleague of Kenneth. 'Larry is our planning manager,' said Kenneth. 'He's been planning a big project since he got here two years ago. That's almost finished and it's time for him to go home.' Larry explained that business was at a peak. He feared that his project would be scuttled by a downturn next year. The time to plan such projects is in the lean years, he said, but no one wants to look at investment abroad then. 'Don't feel too bad about it, my friend,' said Kenneth. 'Projects have been shelved before. Your real task was to create the illusion that the company is committed to new regional investment beyond the minor expansion of a couple of old plants. You have served that purpose well.' Kenneth paused. 'Look at the economics,' he went on. 'You take a plant that was fully depreciated ten years ago. Add valves here, a few pipes there, and *voilà*: you de-bottleneck the capacity of a virtually obsolete plant by 15 per cent.' Larry had obviously heard it all before and excused himself to make a phone call. 'Larry had high hopes when he came here,' said Kenneth. 'The first time we went out together he told me the story of three stonecutters. "Someone asks what they were doing. The first says he is earning a living. The second says he is being a great stonecutter. But the third is a born visionary—he's convinced he is building a cathedral!" Larry used to be a cathedral builder, too. The Asian experience has made him a realist. Now he's just a good stonecutter like the rest of us.'

The latest corporate cliché is 'empowering' the employees, which means nothing more than the good old-fashioned concept of delegation of authority. There are bosses who delegate and bosses who don't. Managers can live with both types so long as they know where they stand. Their nightmare is working for a boss who *thinks* he has delegated everything but in reality has kept all the power tightly in his grasp. He would like his theoretical deputies to operate as if they had a blank cheque to make decisions in their fields of responsibility. At the same time, he makes sure that they constantly read his lips. He is irritated when they seem spineless, but intolerant if they are firm. Such a chief can do more harm to the morale of an organisation than someone who makes no pretence about sharing power—though in both cases the prospects of developing effective managers are close to nil. People working in such a schizoid corporate culture are naturally unhappy. They know that because their company has launched a campaign for empowering employees, their boss pays daily lip service to it. But he continues to control by suspicion and communicate by reprimand. He forgets that the cardinal principle of delegation is trust, and that without that managers feel they work *for* the boss rather than *with* him. They find it hard to develop faith in the company's new culture.

Masters and mentors

The emphasis on power in corporate cultures turns managers into masters rather than mentors. But coaching and guiding motivates people more powerfully than finding fault and giving orders. Expatriate managers in particular can enrich their relationships with Asian employees by being resources rather than bosses. It is so easy for a new manager to arrive from Europe or the USA and lapse into the role of heir to the taipans and nabobs of old. Most Asian societies have attributed to foreigners collectively a status and distinction beyond what an individual may deserve. But today such surface recognition disappears if the individual fails to earn respect on his own merit. A relationship cannot be based on a residue of history. That only demotivates employees and makes the manager a vulnerable caricature. For example, Richard Garner, a new arrival in Asia, was put in charge of a department of ten people. He was not used to the substantial perks his company offered to expatriate employees. Nor was he accustomed to a maid saying 'Garner residence' every time he called home. The fawning and flattery at work went to his head. Richard became a master, intolerant of others who had been on the job much longer than he, ordering them to change to ways familiar to him. He so discouraged the employees that they lost their enthusiasm for cooperating. As a result—though not because of any deliberate plot—a crucial deadline was missed. The delay seriously damaged Richard's career.

Mentors are good at assigning roles commensurate with an employee's background and experience. Gradually, they stretch the responsibility, keeping a friendly eye on progress. They know employees will willingly undertake more difficult duties if supervisors are not unduly demanding or critical. They never insist that there is only one correct way of doing things. They make employees feel the task is a shared responsibility. They have a knack of understanding people's ambitions and linking them with corporate achievements. It is not hard to learn how to be a mentor. The rewards—both in personal satisfaction and corporate recognition—can be high. When I look back over the years, I find that a great number of managers I knew when they were in the middle ranks and who are today at the top of their companies were mentors. They all knew how to make people willingly give their best. Unlike Richard Garner, they did not believe that fear is the prime motivator and rank the only measure of respect. All of them, however, were helped by the positive corporate cultures of their companies.

Personal power

Managers enjoy several powers that flow directly from the positions they hold. They have the power to reward, to recommend promotion, or to approve a raise. The reverse of that is the power to punish, to fire, or to transfer an employee. According to the level of their positions, managers have authority to approve expenditures or sign contracts up to a certain limit. In addition, there are two personal sources of power. The first derives from expertise, knowledge, and practical experience. The second is won by the manager because colleagues admire him, want to emulate him, or are won over by his personality and charm.

The ideal corporate culture is the one in which managers gain respect and influence because of their personal qualities rather than their rank and position. The raw use of power in a multicultural work environment is the single most dangerous way to handle a difficult situation, both on an individual and corporate level. There are numerous instances when such use of power has led to a string of individual resignations or industrial strife.

In these days of participatory management, the very attributes that once put the boss on a pedestal have become a rich source of satire. The tough boss is caricatured daily in a hundred different ways. Ellen Nevins provides a puckish diagnosis of this comic character in her book *Real Bosses Don't Say Thank You*. Real bosses, she explains, aren't wimps. They can boast of distinctive qualities setting them apart from the 'plain vanilla' variety. They never give any reasons for their decisions. Rarely do they delegate any real authority. Their performance evaluation system is practical: the frequency with which one of the employees agrees or disagrees with them says a great deal about that person's judgment and discretion. Three decades ago Douglas McGregor wrote his celebrated work *The Human Side of Enterprise* to prove his thesis that the implicit assumptions a business holds about making use of its human resources determine its whole character. Since then, the military as a metaphor for management structure in business has come increasingly under fire. The preferred analogies today—sailing, playfulness, space stations—certainly help to encourage new ideas about managing, but they often appear too threatening and democratic to authority-devoted managements.

Many large companies, however, are busy these days examining their hierarchical structures. To conduct such a review, Westbig Corporation invited executives from its far-flung operations to a worldwide meeting. Among the last to be converted to the need for change was Herb Moser, vice president for Asia. His panicky, strident tones resounded in the ears of the assembled company. 'Those small traders in Asia are eating our lunch. While we go through our normal layers of management to reach decision, Chang & Co. delivers the product to the customer.' Around the table, managers who had spent the better part of their lives happily mired down in the old system nodded hesitantly. They were aware of a new mood in the boardroom to make the company more responsive to the marketplace. In pleading for a 'flattening', as he put it, of the organisation, Moser

was indirectly expressing the frustration of his Asian colleagues
with company hierarchy. A number had quit to take top jobs with
medium-sized local firms and were now successfully competing with
their old company. But removing hierarchy, inherent in a global
organisation, has little chance of success because it flies squarely
in the face of prophets of gigantism. How can it be effective when
it is being implemented by the same people who are afflicted with
globalmania?

Corporate cavemen

These companies are realising that they cannot change their corporate
culture by simply eliminating a couple of organisational layers or
closing down one or two offices. Their managers are trained to create
barriers that partition off one group of employees from another.
Segregation is justified by the nature of work involved: different
products, different market segments, different activities. On the face
of it these divisions seem logical. But the passion for sub-dividing,
very often, is an organisational malady called the corporate compart-
mentalisation syndrome. The territorial instinct, of course, is fundamental to human nature and can be observed in the imperatives of
tribal society as much as in the modern management ego. Therefore,
it may not be so strange to see global managers turning into corporate
cavemen when the reduced hierarchy creates a diffused proprietary
right over subordinates. Their craving for personal allegiance takes
amusing forms.

When Westbig restructured its Asian operations, the objective,
ostensibly, was to get closer to customers. The declared intention was
to do away with hierarchy. Abolished were the positions of Asian
president and executive vice president, who were replaced with
five tribal chiefs, each head of their own corporate clan. Overnight,
loyalty to the company was fragmented. Employees suffered a
crisis of identity. They had been colleagues, sharing common aspirations, but now they felt diminished. Heads of groups began acting
like presidents of new smaller companies. The common bond provided by top management had disappeared—and with it the most
critical factor in making various divisions work effectively.

In the absence of such a bond, managers tend to work at cross-
purposes. Nowhere is the damage more harmful than in the separa-
tion of marketing and manufacturing functions, especially when taken
to an extreme. Managers become possessive. Ego reigns supreme and
the general corporate interest is forsaken. Khun Samporn, general
marketing manager for the Thai subsidiary of an international company, told me about a recent incident illustrating this. His company

had built a new factory and its top executives had come out for the official opening. But since marketing and manufacturing operations were strictly separated, the expatriate factory manager was solely responsible for the arrangements. 'What is the purpose of a factory if not to sell its products?' lamented Somporn. 'This could have been a valuable occasion for marketing.' The problem lay in the absence of any interlocking relationship between the two subsidiaries—there was no chief executive to integrate the operations. The factory manager reported directly to the manufacturing vice president at the head office. Somporn reported to the Asian regional office. The factory manager was higher in the hierarchy. If Somporn had had his way, there would have been an impressive display of products at the ceremony. There would be a permanent showroom for visitors. But this idea did not go down well with the factory manager. Global companies are realising that every time they remove a top layer, they divide employees rather then bind them together. The culture of maintaining power through barriers is difficult to destroy when the essential spirit of the global organisation is to manage by bureaucracy rather than by building bridges.

Restructuring, carried out in the name of the much touted search for excellence, failed to achieve efficiency. Nor has it brought these companies closer to customers. They used to be amused by the Japanese workers singing company songs and doing morning callisthenics. Surely there were other more effective ways of achieving excellence, they had thought. But restructuring divided their employees into winners and losers. Winners graduated to the inner circle, while the rest nursed their wounds. It will take years, probably decades, for some of these companies to regain the trust of their employees. In Asia especially—where return on investment, growth, and prospects are more impressive—cutting staff to cut costs was not an imperative.

An American banker in Hong Kong puts it this way: 'Reorganisation destroyed camaraderie. Credibility was shattered by changes not necessary for survival.' One result will be the dwindling of the Asian experience at the head office. 'Those close to the power base have done well. Managers over here were forgotten.' Among employees aged 45 to 55, rancour is intense. There was a lot of talk about 'redeployment' but nothing much happened. Says John Neumann, a consultant, 'There's a very, very long list of things you can do, should do, without firing people. Most companies try only one or two and then go for early retirement.' When will top managers learn? Two thousand years ago the Roman satirist Petronius called reorganisation 'a wonderful method for creating the illusion of progress while producing confusion, inefficiency, and demoralisation'.

Serving society

Nor have the efforts of these companies to spread a new corporate culture through global electronic transmission and the distribution of plexiglass mission statements been any more effective. To be successful, corporate cultures must be blended with local cultures and spread by local managements. Paying mere lip service to deeply held cultural values does little good. Those values must be embodied in everyday behaviour. The corporate culture should be seen to serve the interests of society and the economic wellbeing of a country. 'There must be a broader social profit in whatever business we do,' says Yukta Na Thalang, chairman of SGV & Co. in Thailand. He is the country's doyen of accounting and auditing and holds professional registration No.1. He looks on his duties as president of the Thai Chamber of Commerce and Board of Trade, as adviser to the Board of Investment, and as treasurer of a royal foundation, as opportunities to serve. His former employees are now found in almost every industry in Thailand. He regards the investment in their training as a contribution to the country's economic development. 'We are Thai,' he states simply, 'and we must help Thai companies to grow so that we can grow with them.'

The challenge for multinational companies in Asia is to help make material progress compatible with cultural values. More and more Asian managers are realising that a total compromise of values only leads to hollow lives, unrelated to any sense of fulfilment, unconnected with any individual or national pride. Money? Yes, but it must be part of a bigger dream or we end up like my friend Somchai, a Thai manager working with a multinational corporation in Bangkok. Standing in the garden of his beautiful home, he points to his dinner guests, most of whom are successful managers with large companies. 'What's it all about?' he asks me. 'What are they looking for? Are they happy, do you think?' Not far from us, one of the ladies is showing off her Burmese ruby brooch. The women are chatting about their jewellery, neatly pinning down the level of each husband. After the guests are gone, Somchai stands by the pond, the way he had done as a child holding his father's hand. He looks at the moon's reflection and an emptiness takes hold of him. His life, he thinks, is but a poor reflection of the idealistic dreams of his youth. He knows his international company values him as a great stonecutter. But he has never experienced the exaltation of being a cathedral builder.

Setting an example

Somchai also feels bitterly that he is not a role model even to his children. Back when he was a young manager, looking up to role models used be natural. Today's generation, he feels, are surrounded by shattered idols. No sphere of life seems immune. He told me the tale of Vidya, an intelligent young graduate of Chulalongkorn university. A well-known *farang* journalist she had long admired was invited to attend an evening function in Bangkok. Vidya was excited at the prospect of meeting him. He was intellectually fearless, she felt, and she hoped one day to write like that herself. The evening did turn out to be memorable—but not in the way she had envisaged. The banquet hall was full of celebrities—leading businessmen, politicians, and academics. Vidya found herself sitting at the great man's table. She noticed he was drinking heavily and that his conversation was erratic. He stumbled past some tables to ask the beautiful wife of a Thai politician to dance. They had hardly reached the floor when, to Vidya's horror, the famous writer stumbled and almost fell flat on his face. That was the end of him as a role model for Vidya.

Ikram is another young person who also finds himself sadly disillusioned. He had just joined a large insurance company in Kuala Lumpur. His expatriate department manager had taken him under his wing and Ikram told two senior Malaysian colleagues how much he admired his boss. But in a matter of months, the department manager had taken on more trainees and fired the two older Malaysians. 'It didn't take me long to realise he had no loyalty to his team. He was cutting costs by replacing higher-paid executives with younger ones. To him, we were just cheap labour,' says the unhappy young man.

Vidya and Ikram are just two examples of Asian young folk finding it hard to live without idols. Our youth still hungrily devour books about the world's successful men and women. They have been brought up to emulate, to build their lives on familiar patterns. Asian corporate culture must create its own meaningful role models for our youth.

Kunio Yoshihara makes a disturbing point in his book *The Rise of Ersatz Capitalism in Southeast Asia*. Indigenous capitalism in the region, he says, is only in the service sector. People who control these enterprises are cronies and compradores. Many of them became capitalists because they were the children of political leaders or had close connections with bureaucrats. They want to acquire monopolies, special licenses, subsidies, and other special favours from government. Therefore, Kunio questions their ability for self-growth. He points out that a more serious problem of the growth of capitalism and industrialisation in the region is that it is not inspired by technology. Most entrepreneurs came from the merchant capitalist class and have little understanding of, or interest in, the technological aspects of their companies.

However, the achievements of many modern businessmen disprove Kunio's claim. Taiwan's Stan Shih is an example. In a span of fourteen years, he has developed his Acer group from a mere $25 000 and eleven employees into a major conglomerate in the field of information systems. Says Shih: 'The direction of our corporate culture is determined by the needs of our people and the needs of the company. We relate these needs to some concepts in Chinese history and culture, so that the corporate culture is more easily understood and practiced by our employees.' Shih's words could equally apply to several other successful Asian companies who are benefiting from a mix of their society's old culture and modern technology. Their corporate culture is not based on a passing fad but on the durable foundation of collective mission and pride.

9   Corporate communication: global versus local

It is often said that management is the art of communication. And yet its poor quality is the most pervasive problem in a majority of multinational corporations. Despite the telecommunications explosion of recent years, it is debatable whether modern executives are any more effective in conveying their messages than primitive man was in using a drum or smoke signal. In their zeal for instant communication, many executives have let the medium become the message. They marvel at their ability to transmit a thousand words per second around the globe, but they don't pause to think about the cultural decoding of these messages by the recipients in different countries.

Communication phases

The last three or four decades have seen several phases of corporate communication. At one time 'no comment' was the most frequent response in external communications: the less said the better about that dismal phase.

Low profile

Then came 'low profile' which was considered more imaginative: it conceded that a company may on occasion have to comment on its activities. This was, however, considered a non-productive exercise, to be undertaken without detracting from the main task of making and selling products or providing a service. Management remained convinced that the general public was too unsophisticated to understand the complexities of business. There was a taint of pseudo-sophistication in this approach. Low profile did not exclude promoting the image of executives as long as they didn't talk too much about business. When Westbig Corporation decided to move its Asia-Pacific head office from New York to Hong Kong, a leading American industrial magazine carried a profile of Jeremy Pickle, the executive designated to head the regional operations. Under a full-page headline, declaring 'Connecticut Yankee tackles the Far-Eastern market', the article provided a remarkable glimpse of the man who was to lead the company's growth in Asia. It read:

> The new president leans back a bit precariously in a wooden armchair propping his feet up on a coffee table in his New York office one afternoon before his move. He emphasises points by jabbing the air with his reading glasses and tugging at his red-figured dark-blue tie...the 43-year old executive, at 6-foot 4 and 200 lbs, has the look of an athlete (he was a track man in his college days). The president's new home in Hong Kong is a rented, Western-style, three-storey house perched on a cliff, as most of the Hong Kong homes are.

Thousands of Asian employees who read the article were none the wiser about the company's plans for the region. They were to learn, however, from another interview in a prestigious international business magazine that, after the move from New York, their new boss had developed a serious problem. In just two months he made seven transpacific flights and had become a chronic victim of jet-lag. He felt irritable, his eyes itched, and he couldn't read much. Then he decided to have a complete physical check-up. 'What you need are a couple of bowls of snake soup,' said the company doctor who took the new president to a snake shop. 'You know, it really calmed me down,' the president confided in an exclusive interview to the magazine.

High profile

This colourful phase of communications did little to help the image of business, particularly that of large companies. In December 1975, the Opinion Research Corporation reported that fewer people had high trust and confidence in large companies than in any of the fourteen other institutions in American society. It remarked that, in the wake of the post-Watergate stream of publicity about political payoffs at home and illegal bribes abroad, big business had at no time since the days of the imperious robber barons been more vulnerable to attack. It added:

> Indeed, the situation is such that, to survive and prosper in today's increasingly hostile attitude and climate, large companies, if not already doing so, simply are going to have to redefine their role and responsibility in society. No longer is it simply enough for large companies to devote themselves solely to economic goals. The large company must recognise that it has a larger constituency than its stockholders.

Faced with such a situation, the corporate world decided that the time had come to fight back. It pronounced that the biggest problem hindering business was the lack of effective communication. The era of high profile was well and truly launched.

No direct link was made between poor image and the actions and performance of business. While the public was clamouring for business to change some of its practices, no one examined whether certain things really needed changing. It was simply believed that the solution lay in better communication of old ways. Joseph Nolan, professor of journalism and public affairs at the University of South Carolina, said in an article in the *Harvard Business Review*, 'While constantly lamenting the lowly standing of the "business image", businessmen themselves are so preoccupied with the communication and cosmetic dimensions of their problems that they tend to overlook everything else.' M.A. Wright, chairman of Exxon, USA, echoed the conventional wisdom of a generation of his corporate colleagues when he declared that 'business has failed to do an effective job in communicating its point of view to the general public'.

On occasion there was just a hint of acceptance of the real problems. In a videotaped interview called *A View from the Top*, the chairman of a large multinational was asked about the most difficult problem affecting his company abroad. 'The question is, how do you satisfy the government and the public of another country that an American company will do what is in their best interest?' he replied. 'Our managers overseas are constantly being called upon to demonstrate and to indicate to governments and public why it is that we, an American company, can do the job for them that they need and why they want to keep us there. And that's a constant challenge.'

Global communication

That challenge was resolved later, at least in the minds of large companies, when they started calling themselves multinational—which brings us to the current phase called global communication. The restructuring and reorganisation through which most of the large multinationals have gone during the last few years was the major inspiration for this phase. Since the ostensible justification for the massive restructuring was to compete in the emerging single world market, the only way to handle corporate communications, both internally and externally, was to go global.

Enter the experts hired by multinationals to tour the world to train local managers in handling media. Their presentations are polished and slick, but their approach, terminology, and examples are borrowed from other places, other people. To them, the media is an adversary—confrontational, hostile, even unethical. A video shows a warm-up session, before a TV interview, with a consultant advising his client, a cigarette company, not to answer any hypothetical questions. The message is: don't trust the media; they are out to get you. One can't blame the participating Asian managers for forming a pretty poor impression of television and newspaper people. However, business coverage in our media is non-confrontational. So why introduce a neurosis born of a different cultural environment? These consultants with their videotaped media crises seem to be saying, 'But for us this could happen to you, too.' They cannot shake the siege mentality. What's the point in showing clips of business executives hounded by sensation-seeking TV journalists, when we don't have those kinds of shows?

Instead of combative training, we need to encourage businessmen to talk freely about their operations, to build trust, promote confidence, and encourage faith in the future. They should hold periodic press seminars to brief journalists on the progress of their companies and the state of the industry. They should meet at relaxed informal briefings, not only under the stress of short-notice formal interviews.

Advertising

Advertising is another powerful way in which business communicates with customers and the general public. Here again, the global technique so often overwhelms the need to convey a simple local message. The local affiliate of a multinational company in Singapore once invited advertising proposals from two agencies, one large and the other small. At the review by the company's management committee, the big outfit presented its stuff with a great fanfare and emphasised the professional excellence of their visuals and copy. Indeed, the promoters were fully confident that more than one advertisement in the campaign would prove worthy of an international award. Then came the small agency: two young men with a handful of rough sketches and simple, straightforward copy. The vote was overwhelmingly in favour of the large company. Looking around the table, the veteran chief executive, intimate with the Asian cultural scene, asked each manager to explain their preference. In most cases they preferred the greater 'technical' competence of the polished professionals. 'Did any of you feel that the message in their proposed campaign was contrived?' he asked. The manufacturing director agreed, but thought there was something of that in all advertising. The chief executive persisted: 'Put yourself in the position of local customers. Would they intuitively trust those ads because they are more skilfully executed? As a large international company, do we need superficial imagery or do we want a simple home-grown message like the one the two young men presented?'

Time and again we run into similar situations. So often is the soul of a message lost by sacrificing simplicity, its effectiveness destroyed by gadgetry and the sophisticated devices used to convey it—especially by global experts who don't know Asia. Advertising is like a window on a culture. It offers us dramatic glimpses of the social values of a nation. Therefore it is often easy for a global advertisement to offend the values of Asian consumers. Language, symbols, signs, and choice of models can lead to different interpretations and meanings of the same visual message. Historical and traditional beliefs, superstition, and preferences for certain colours demand different treatments. Advertising that identifies itself with national traits is usually more effective. But the result can often be stereotyped when people new to Asia use their superficial knowledge of these traits and project what they *think* Asians believe. The hard sell, for instance, is generally not a very good idea in Asian advertising. Nor is the tendency to claim that your product is better than the competition's. Gentler and subtler ways of persuasion are more acceptable. 'You don't have to speak explicitly in Japanese advertising,' says Inoue Takashi, a strategy analyst and planner at Hakuhodo, Inc., the second-largest advertising agency in the country. He adds:

> Builders in Europe often make houses and streets from stone, which they break and shape by applying great force in one place. But in traditional Japanese houses, we decorate with bamboo, which we wind and bend. If you use too much force, you break the shaft; so you work gradually, and by and by, the bamboo gives way. It is the same in our way of thinking, in our way of living. It is the same in advertising: you work gently, and by and by, the consumer gives way.

I don't wish to devalue the great advances in communication technology, but rather to put them in perspective. Colour television is doubtless more pleasing than black-and-white, but the soap operas that dominate the box today are hardly impressive. If technical competence in their communication made the messages themselves more convincing, we would have less crime, drugs, or AIDS. We may be able to cram the accumulated wisdom of the ages on a computer disk, but whether that would make people any the wiser has yet to be proved. It is too easy to become a slave to modern technology and to regard simpler methods as 'primitive'. Particularly disturbing is the occasional remark by some young global newcomer that PR is a Western art. It's like saying that modern medicine is a Western science. But if you know nothing about tropical diseases and cannot diagnose an illness without a hundred tests, if you don't understand the social context in which you must function, and use technique to camouflage absence of content, you cannot be very effective. My advice to business? Beware of your communications expert who claims to be well up on global techniques but is unable to convey the spirit and purpose of your organisation in a way Asians can relate to and understand.

Personal contacts

Global communications take yet another form which leaves a lot to be desired—the passion for forging personal contacts with senior officials and businessmen around the world. At best this is an exercise in ego satisfaction as it does little to enhance the quality of corporate external relationships. It is often justified on the grounds of gathering first-hand knowledge about the countries where the global corporation operates. It is rarely a serious exercise in understanding political situations. Though politics is crucial to their interests, many big corporations rely on ad hoc judgments instead of on systematic assessments.

Most of the head-office dignitaries are sceptical about local managers as sources of objective information because they believe their views are 'coloured by national interests'. But they themselves are guilty of treating overseas environments as an extension of their situation at home. Often political forecasting is reduced to a social pastime. The game takes the form of 'After Suharto (Aquino, Lee Kuan Yew), who?' Whenever the company president is in town, senior managers arrange 'courtesy calls' on top state officials. This is to make his visit seem more important. But if the president has no real grasp of the political environment, the exercise can misfire badly. One visiting executive vice president once asked a Singapore minister what he thought of the prime minister. That call was a very short one. The Tokyo manager of another big company was aghast when his head office directed him to arrange a call on the prime minister during the chairman's trip to Japan in connection with a new joint venture. Since the investment was a mere $20 million and in no way contentious, the Japanese could see no point in meeting. A director of another company was miffed when a minister in a developing country wouldn't let him get a word in. Later he shot down an attractive investment project on the grounds that the government there was disorganised. He hadn't understood the custom of leaving operations to senior civil servants. Another visiting executive, paying a courtesy call on a Malaysian minister, didn't take along the Kuala Lumpur manager who had arranged the meeting. The politician refused to see him without the local man, who had to be urgently summoned. One wonders about the value of head-office executives making these contacts. A Malaysian official recently showed me business cards of eighteen executives from the head office of an international company who had all paid him a courtesy call in connection with a proposed project. Wouldn't it be more effective to leave this activity in the hands of capable local and regional managers?

Any prejudice against nationals and long-time resident expatriates ought to be re-examined, since their optimism is often due not to a lack of objectivity but to a familiarity with the risks involved and a confidence in their own ability to manage them. The further from the scene, the greater the risk appears. Local managers are clearly in the best position to interpret the political environment. They are also in the best position to negotiate without hurting national sensitivities. Global managers can easily make local officials feel like pawns on a colossal chessboard. In dealing with multinationals, local managers are reminded daily that the international game of capital and technology is played by remote control. Sometimes there is a degree of arrogance in the way these games are played. Says Anat Arbhabhirama, governor of the Petroleum Authority of Thailand, 'It's not uncommon for foreign executives to run into government officials who will not do business with them if they don't like the way they behave.'

The monolithic voice

Multinationals must avoid speaking with a monolithic voice and behaving as if the world were a single cultural entity. A statement made in one country may be decoded in an entirely different way in another. A little over ten years ago, a news item was flashed around the world pointing out that the American secretary of treasury at that time had rejected a proposal from Exxon Corporation to 'block' a World Bank program to finance natural gas and petroleum exploration in less-developed countries. It said that the Exxon chairman had appealed to the treasury secretary, who represented the USA on the World Bank's board of governors, to try to convince the bank it should leave the financing of oil and gas exploration to the private sector. According to a bank energy specialist the purpose of the program was to provide less-developed countries with an independent source of information and expert advice that could be used in negotiating with the world energy corporations if evidence of sufficient petroleum and natural gas reserves were discovered. The correspondence between the Exxon chairman and the USA treasury secretary led to widely differing interpretations in different parts of the world. The tone of Exxon's approach with its emphasis on the use of private capital rather than public funds for risky ventures was suited to the American media; in Asia it appeared as an attempt to undermine government programs to develop domestic sources of energy. Such instances remind us every day why multinationals must learn to be multi-local in their communications.

The Asian subsidiaries of multinationals have been subjected to the same phases of communication as those followed by their head offices. But these postures were in reaction to the prevailing relationship between business and society in the USA, and to a lesser degree in Europe. In Asia the first two phases, namely no comment and low profile, covered the post-independence period, a time when business here should have taken an active part in the debate over the formulation of economic policies. That opportunity was lost. Now again the need for greater intra-regional communication is being overlooked due to a preoccupation with the global thrust.

Intra-Asian trade has risen remarkably and should outstrip trans-pacific commerce in ten years. The emergence of protectionist-inclined trading blocs elsewhere could soon make regional cooperation a matter of survival rather than choice. But North America and Europe seem to make a far deeper cultural imprint on Asia than that which our own societies have been able to stamp on one another. Media coverage, books, films, and television programs meant to educate and entertain us remain largely Western-oriented. In the past there was no choice. Asia was Balkanised by colonialism for centuries. We were taught to look on one another with suspicion and distrust. It was fashionable to identify with our rulers more than with our neighbours. Old habits continue to perpetuate this mistaken sense of loyalty. To young Filipinos, Bangkok can seem ten times more distant than Boston. Every nuance of the latest details of Donald and Ivana Trump's marital squabble commands more notice on our evening news than the monumental nation-building task that is taking place all around us.

Internal communication

Let us take a quick look at internal communications and see what has happened to that mighty tool of management—the employee magazine. Out of a recent sample I chose one that's fairly representative. Aimed at the company's 50 000 employees from New York to Hong Kong and from Brussels to Bombay, it's a flagrant exercise in arrogance. Its first article, seemingly written by the chief executive himself and adorned with an imposing portrait of him, stresses the company's total commitment to keeping its employees informed worldwide. The firm is among the many business empires that have been through prolonged throes of restructuring, during which the appearance of their magazines had been spotty or altogether absent. The article makes no apology for keeping its employees in the dark during the most traumatic period of their working lives.

Another article under the heading 'A truly worldwide business' is devoted to glowing accounts of the company's global reach. While the American and European operations are illustrated with photographs of laboratories and industrial plants emphasising the company's technological strength, the Asian portion is highlighted by pictures of Bangkok bars, Peking duck and the hard-back turtles of Malaysia. The crypto-travelogue on the Exotic East introduces the opening of one of the company's most advanced plants in Japan with these words from the president: 'Imagine bringing a new manufacturing plant on-stream, but only after first having a Shinto priest, dressed in ritual vestments, invoke an appropriate blessing.' Then for the cultural edification of his employees worldwide, he adds, 'This is a requisite of any plant dedication in Japan.' The Asian readers, for whom similar ceremonies are a way of life, were not edified. The article does refer to the region's economic boom and raises hopes of hitching the corporate wagon to this star by way of a strategy study group. You would think the company was new to Asia if you didn't know it has been in business here for 75 years. The impersonal style of other articles smacks of feudal lords addressing their estate serfs, rather than the sharing of news among modern managers. No vision of a common purpose and identity emerges beyond the assurance by another dignitary that staff members engaged in their various businesses across the world can be proud that they belong to a single company. As to product quality, job security, contributions to local economies, and broader social and environmental concerns—none of these make an appearance on the glossy pages. Talking about the problems and risks facing an international company, the president cautions that 'the tides of nationalism continue to rise and that business ethics in some countries tolerate practices that are anathema to an American-based firm'.

Other channels of communication

International videos and mission statements, two more modern weapons in the management armoury, are even more provocative. Produced in Hollywood style, the videos may provide an afternoon of entertainment, but highlight the remoteness of top management from far-flung operations. Mission statements detailing corporate strategies and goals are communicated to a relatively small number of managers who have reached a certain level. Instead of achieving cooperation within the company, they create a sense of segregation in the ranks of the employees. Other mission statements, proclaiming that the objective of the company is simply to be the best in its industry, are received with less than enthusiasm. Asian managers are seldom motivated by such abstract statements. Increasing volume by 5 per cent works better as a personally agreed goal. A Malaysian sales manager once told me that his customers didn't care much whether his company was the industry leader or not. They would say to him, 'Ibrahim, we do business with your company because of you.' Ibrahim expected the same chain of personal relationship all the way to the top. He wasn't a bit impressed by a plaque with a declaration of company purpose engraved upon it, signed by a person he'd never met.

Of course, no one dares criticise these internal programs, since the much photographed and filmed elders cite them routinely as examples of their faith in global communication. From the standpoint of employees here, though, they present an unmitigated disaster, painting Asia as a colourful tail wagged by the body of American or European business. In thier newly acquired passion for global communication, these companies don't realise that if they are serious about their commitment to Asia, they could achieve the objective far more effectively by launching regional communication programs and thus conveying the message of earnestness more eloquently. Head-office pronouncements and stories of interest from other regions could always fit in. But chiefly regional programs could dedicate more attention to issues close to the heart of Asian employees—and salute their achievements, now either ignored or buried beneath exaltation of global grandees.

Global programs lull top management into a false sense of comfort. By simply having them, they feel they have served the dictates of modern communication. What is actually communicated, and to what purpose, ceases to matter much. Is it to share business problems and prospects with employees as partners, instil pride, and promote enthusiasm? Is it an honest attempt to build bridges or repair one that may have snapped due to corporate 'rationalisation'? Or is it communication for its own sake: pulpit preaching, self-satisfying piffle? Sadly, the answer is that they are nothing but global garbage. Far from creating understanding, they are giving rise to huge information gaps.

Although activity has proliferated, employees do not believe top managers are interested in dialogue, but only in communicating from the top down. There is no attempt to take into account employee suggestions or to accept the fact that most employees still prefer face-to-face talks. Employees want a stronger communication relationship with their company leaders. Their job satisfaction and performance are greatly influenced by their perception of the sincerity and quality of top management communication. But this must involve listening as well talking. Even when the most effective method of face-to-face communication is used, simply delivering monologues is of little help. An amazingly large number of global executives who think they are good speakers are actually very poor at it. Some are convinced they have to be orators to talk to a group of employees or associates. Others try to imitate politicians or preachers. They don't realise that their slick presentations smack of insincerity. They don't know that Asians dislike hype. Our old friend, Jeremy Pickle, is a prime example of the orator type. He had the 'gift of the gab'. He fancied himself as a good speaker and loved using long, convoluted sentences. He used words to con rather than to convince people. He enjoyed dominating his audience, frequently employing sarcasm to put down those whose questions or comments he did not like. More often than not, he left his listeners bewildered.

Then there is the corporate politician who leaves his Asian listeners bemused. A visiting executive, who had just been put in charge of international operations, announced at his welcome party, 'The only reason I accepted my new job is because my wife and I have always been deeply interested in Asian cultures. At first we were not keen on moving to the Brussels head office, but then we willingly gave up our comfortable home in Toronto as the assignment offers us the opportunity to travel to the Far East.' A couple of Asian managers discovered how shallow the man's interest was when, the very next day, he impatiently dismissed as irrelevant a brief outline of social and cultural values included in the preamble to a marketing presentation.

The worst executive of all, however, is the preacher type, reeking of dishonesty even as he imagines everybody believes him. 'We are going to reorganise our business, but I am here to give you my personal assurance that we will do everything in our power to make sure no one is hurt,' he declares. 'To those of you we have to let go, I want to say that I am available day and night to listen to your problems. Just call me at head office at 233–605–2782. God bless you.' So wrapped in his own oratory was this man that he did not notice the looks of derision directed towards him.

To be successful in Asia in the future, multinationals will have to respond to the region's unique communication styles and needs—both external and internal. In the tough times ahead they are likely to discover with a shock that global communication is a poor recipe for survival.

10 The social responsibility of business

On a bright sunny November afternoon in 1989, as I drove past the house in New Delhi where I had once lived for several years, I was struck by the size of the eucalyptus tree in the garden. It was just a sapling when I had planted it almost 25 years ago. During the few minutes on my way to the Ashok hotel, where I had an appointment with His Holiness the Dalai Lama, I felt gratified that the new occupants were enjoying the result of a small effort on my part long ago. There are so few acts in life, I thought, that give us a sense of sharing.

As I pressed the button to the Dalai Lama's floor, I recalled meeting Krishna Menon many years ago in the same lift. He had at that time just resigned as defence minister but still represented the ruling Congress party's left wing. I had reminded him that we had met once before abroad and that I was now back in India. He had asked me what I did. When I told him I worked for Esso (Exxon), he responded with a wry smile, 'I'm sure they pay you well.' That parting remark, its tone almost suggesting that I was guilty of something immoral, was still echoing in my ears when I was ushered into the Dalai Lama's suite.

The world as a whole

After a brief introduction, I found myself asking His Holiness whether he thought moral values were incompatible with material progress. 'I don't think so. My belief is that moral values such as compassion, love, altruism, forgiveness, and sincerity, are not just moral attributes. They are something that's necessary or compulsory in life,' replied the Dalai Lama. 'If you look at a particular economic field, you may not see any relevance,' he said. 'But if you look at the world as a whole or as one entity, then you have to ask, economic activity for whom? Certainly not economy for God, not economy for animals, but mainly for human beings. So, in every field I feel it's extremely important to have a clear recognition of the importance of human beings. Without that we may face disaster.'

The cynical view, I said, was that to get on in life you have to compromise your moral values. His Holiness replied with a warm smile:

> Often it appears that if you are too much concerned about others, you may not be able to maximise profit. If you take advantage of others at every opportunity, regardless of its effect on them, you may gain more productivity. A particular family may gain much more profit, but at the same time it may create more enemies, hurt more people, create complaints, negative attitudes, and feelings. A few individual rich families getting wealthier, and at the same time in the same community people still remaining poor. Then ultimately there is social unrest.

After a moment's pause, he added: 'If you think only of immediate profit then naturally we have to use all the resources of the planet in a maximum way. In that case the long-term consequences are obvious. The next generation will face imbalances. Therefore, unless you look at the overall situation, there could be serious problems.' How were we going to bring about this awareness? Education, he replied.

> For example, the North and South differences: the industrialised nations make profit in a way which intentionally or unintentionally involves some kind of exploitation of the South. As a result there is a conflict. We must think of the long-term consequences of these factors. Also, some big industries are only concerned with making profit. Then they face serious pollution problems. They have to spend much money in order to protect people. Once the environment is polluted, the wealthier people also face the same problems. They are part of the community.

Did that mean economic activity and moral life could not be segregated? I asked. His Holiness explained:

> There is a social power for human happiness in the long run. Any activity—economic, technological, scientific—every field of human activity is basically carried out by human beings and meant for human beings. So when we talk about human benefit as the rationale of this activity, then the foundation is love. The human body itself, besides mind consciousness, needs others' affection. A child, even before birth in the mother's womb, is very much affected by the mother's mental condition. Then, after the birth, the next few weeks, according to scientists (especially brain scientists), are a crucial period for the development of the brain. During that period, simply the mother's physical touch is crucial. So you see, one of the basic human needs is

affection. If human activity is isolated from basic human feelings, then technology and science will bring disaster to humanity.

I said that there are people who talk about economic man in isolation of everything else. The so-called scientific management sought to treat human beings like any other machine in the process of production. His reaction was emphatic:

> That I think is dangerous. Very dangerous. One of the reasons why people in many communist countries are becoming unhappy is that, although the basic goal of the state is maximum benefit for working-class people and the highest prosperity, the way they achieve it is by sacrificing human rights. With that kind of system or ideology they give very little value to individual or human life. As a result tragedies happen. In the economic field, one of the foundations of exploitation is ownership by families who are making profit and who regard the workers simply as a means of making money. The basis of exploitation is inadequate human feeling.
>
> If we look at some of the Japanese companies, their profits are good. Why? Because of the relations between the workers and the companies. The company takes full responsibility for the individual and provides for future security. Because of that situation, each individual worker faithfully works for the company. So there is good cooperation. As a result the company gains much profit. In the other case, if the workers are simply exploited and are not satisfied, production is affected and is of poor quality.

Is the world heading towards a catastrophe? I asked. Are we waiting for a spiritual retribution for humanity's greed? 'I don't know,' he smiled. Do you believe in spiritual punishment? I persisted. 'The Buddhists believe in punishment in the sense of one's own past wrong actions only,' he replied. Did he mean actions in a previous life? 'Not necessarily, actions also in this life. If you did some wrong action yesterday or last year, you may face the consequences this year. That kind of thing happens—at both levels, the obvious level and the more mysterious one.' Did that happen to societies as well? 'Society is common action. Due to previous common action there is later a common suffering, common experience.' Could it happen to the whole planet? 'Yes, that's possible,' replied his Holiness. Finally I asked if His Holiness had a message for business people. 'I believe business people are among the influential members of the human community. So they are very much relevant to peace and prosperity. Sometimes I feel that business people not thinking about others is bad, but even worse are those who produce weapons and try to sell them to innocent people. We need less ammunition, less weapons, less guns, less killings.'

The decade of greed

I reflected on these thoughts as I took a stroll in the Diplomatic Enclave, the capital's most beautiful residential area. Without moral underpinning, would the economic façade come crumbling down some day? The decade, I thought, will be remembered as the era of quick and easy money. Will there be a retribution on a grand economic scale? Perhaps the Dalai Lama was right. Though many heroes of the 1980s have fallen from grace, their philosophy of 'get rich quick' has by no means lost its lustre. Ivan Boesky summed it up in his 1985 address to graduates of the University of California Business School: 'Greed is all right. Greed is healthy. You can be greedy and still feel good about yourself.'

George Goodman, author of *The Roaring '80s*, writing under his pen name of Adam Smith, says American economic history has a certain ebb and flow. Periods of riches—their gathering, spending, and display—end by success leading to excess, bringing terms of penance. William Simon, a former American treasury secretary, sees it as a curative cycle. He feels that if inflation heats up, or a recession hits, a lot of debt-laden companies will be in deep trouble. Smith agrees that debt is the main danger. The Reagan years added roughly $1 trillion to the American national debt, a sum equal to all of what the republic ran up in its first 200 years. Debt grew faster than the gross national product for more than a decade, much faster than corporate profits and equity. The total of all household, government, and business obligations rose from $1.2 trillion in 1970 to $8 trillion in 1987.

Debt also loomed large in leveraged buy-outs in the 1980s. Junk bond purveyors earned fees in millions of dollars for a few days' work. Brain power and talent flocked to paper manipulation instead of the hard work of manufacturing. Ben Stein, a Los Angeles columnist, warned that Wall Street and the leveraged buy-out phenomenon were turning American industry into a vast junkyard of corporate spare parts. Earlier pioneers made fortunes, but first they had to invent things, build factories, staff them with engineers, and develop large organisations to distribute and sell their products. In contrast, the paper fortunes of the 1980s took neither time nor special credit-worthiness.

Making millions today is easier than ever before, says Robert Heller, in his book *The Age of the Common Millionaire*. Creating money once meant creating an equivalent amount in assets. But modern operators like Ted Turner (who issued $1.4 billion in junk bonds to buy MGM alone) discovered that wealth reflecting real assets could be gained with no assets at all. High indebtedness is one of their hallmarks. Hence the rise of men such as John Elliott, Robert Holmes à Court, and Alan Bond. Kemmons Wilson of Holiday Inns fame loved to say that he never wanted to own a million dollars but to owe it. Turner even boasted, 'I've got more debt than anyone in the world. That's something, isn't it?'

A lot of tycoons were in the right place at the right time, such as oil potentates and their advisors. Many hundreds of others found an easy road to millionairedom by way of taking small, often obscure, private businesses into semi-public ownership. Heller expresses concern that such ploys may endanger social stability by widening the gulf between rich and poor. Like the Medici and Gonzaga families of old, today's merchant princes may buy grand houses and otherwise consume lavishly, but also 'like the *palazzi* of the Renaissance princes, the Common Millionaires' houses are built on the sand of their society.' Some rational system is needed, Heller concludes, under which society rewards people more in proportion to the value they contribute to it.

Social purpose

Asian societies do have a system that weighs material success in a traditional scale before rewarding it with recognition and respect. Once I was at a sports club with my friend, Joe Tsang. We were joined by a mutual acquaintance by the name of Greg, an expatriate manager with a foreign firm. Suddenly spotting a well-known multimillionaire at the next table, Greg quietly drew our attention to his presence with a distinct reverence in his whisper. I couldn't help noticing his surprise at Joe's reaction. 'A few years ago he was selling fish in the local market,' Joe spat out. Joe's tone of dismissal stopped Greg from pursuing the matter, but he obviously wondered why Joe had heaped scorn on the business tycoon.

People look down upon the wealthy because they discern an absence of a social purpose in their lives. They see it as acquisition of wealth for wealth's sake: a mere personal obsession, not an activity that creates jobs, nurtures prosperity, and leads to higher standards of health and education. To them, what's important isn't the size of anyone's fortune but the sharing of a collective purpose, the kind of spirit perceptible in countries like Japan and Singapore. The sense of a common mission—survival, prosperity, national pride—almost mystically makes people believe in success and endorse it. Simply getting rich, no matter how much ingenuity and enterprise goes into it, can buy influence but not respect. For that, it must be seen to be in step with a wider purpose. In Japan, many businessmen and industrialists are closely identified by the public with their national economic fortunes. One could cite similar cases elsewhere in Asia, but only a few. These are the people who command respect from everyone, including my friend Joe, because from humble beginnings, such as selling fish in the local market, they went on to build a fishing industry for their country. Similarly, to be honoured, corporate success must be related to national purpose.

Several powerful forces are currently working to the advantage of the developing world. One is the internationalisation of labour and capital. The other is the shift from ideology to pragmatism resulting from the demise of the Cold War. Caught up in the confrontation between the superpowers, many developing countries found themselves ideological pawns in the Cold War. Their approach to economic and political development was conditioned more by allegiance to one or the other bloc than by the need to harness national talents. It led to tortured patterns of thought and leadership. Basic human rights were deprived on the pretext of protecting freedom. People who yearned for democracy were called communists on the one hand and reactionaries on the other. But now ideology is no longer the driving force for national development.

On the economic front, the new order will call for the liberalisation of policies, concentration on building infrastructure, and the integration of foreign investment into the mainstream of national economies. On the political front, it will demand statesmanship to respond to people power. With no one to blame for undermining their plans, leaders of developing countries will be judged on their ability to manage domestic affairs. They will have to find indigenous solutions to their problems, choosing or adapting from other places such courses of action as seem likely to work and not just doing what is expected of them. Productive use of human resources will be their biggest challenge, and policies will have to meet it or be abandoned.

Both as an economic and a moral force, Asia will make a much greater impact on history in the next 50 years than in the past five centuries. Its slums and benighted villages will pose a challenge to reason and conscience, not present a contest for ideology. It will be an era of unprecedented opportunity, but it will also call for broader social responsibility on the part of business.

Enlightened self-interest

A recent editorial in *Asiaweek* pointed to the danger that, with the retreat of communism, ideologues of unfettered capitalism may overlook the concept of social responsibility:

> The danger is acute in Asia, where inequalities of income and opportunity remain wide despite dramatic gains in prosperity overall.

Asian business and industry have to recognise now that they need to address such problems voluntarily. If capitalism is truly to triumph, it will have to fulfil those promises on which communism failed to deliver... The old notion that social conscience is a 'wet' philosophy indulged in by offbeat do-gooders is an alibi. Another excuse is that private interests cannot really solve anything. There are probably a handful of people in Manila who could make life tangibly better for every Filipino by next Thursday if they wanted.

Most Asian companies are decades behind their Western counterparts in accepting the concept of social responsibility. Almost twenty years ago, Exxon developed a document on the subject which stated that the environment of business was in flux. New voices were asking critical questions about business performance and the proper role of the corporation. 'No economic system is God-given: corporations exist at the pleasure of society; the charter evolves as the society evolves,' the document added. It offered the concept of enlightened self-interest as an answer. '*Enlightened* self-interest is responsive to basic shifts in public attitudes (it is the wise bamboo which bends with the wind), consistently sensitive to human values, alert to subtle and indirect effects, and long in view. It is responsive to increasing expectations of openness and accountability. In sum, it seeks to take into account the interest of others. But in the final analysis it is still self-interest.'

The relationship between business and society has changed dramatically in the last few decades. Corporate aid to arts and education is an example. In Asia, though, this is miniscule compared with what international companies spend at home. The perception seems to be that business in Asia today is what it was in the West a century ago. Executives are not aware of, or don't care about, the social consequences of such a belief. Asian managers are pragmatic but not devoid of idealism. Says Banchong Somboonpakorn, manager of Thai Chemicals: 'When you graduate, you have a sense of idealism. Then you get married and have to look after your family. But in your fifties you want to contribute to society or the nation.' Great enterprises are often built by people with a deep sense of social change. Companies ought to do an occasional social audit of how their business helps society's aims and how their growth helps achieve broader aspirations.

Privatisation

Businessmen should also actively participate in economic discussions. Take privatisation, for instance, which is enjoying a burst of popularity today. It is obviously a good trend for Asia. But it might not prove to be a cure for all economic ills, particularly if there is not enough discussion to make people aware of its significance. Attila Karaosmanoglu, the World Bank's vice president for Asia, told me how important he thought it was to carry out privatisation with the utmost care rather than just blindly follow the trend. He recommends three guidelines to make sure the process is successful. First, a 'transparency' in its introduction. It must be perceived by the public as the right thing to do. That means explaining the purpose openly so that it may be judged on its merits. Second is equity. It should be seen as a fair deal in which everyone can participate. If people feel that only a few stand to benefit, it will fail. The third principle is efficiency. 'There is no point in shifting a public monopoly to a private monopoly,' says Karaosmanoglu. 'In operations where you cannot avoid a monopoly, the government must develop a regulatory framework to protect the public interest.' Plans should also look to shifting any labour made redundant to other gainful work. Rushing into privatisation without consulting the people who have the most to lose will provoke resentment.

Unfortunately, the general crisis of confidence in leadership that some countries suffer makes every change in policy be regarded as suspect. It is seen as a pretext for individual or partisan gain. One of the great tragedies of post-independent Asia is that its political leaders have had little business or managerial expertise. The fight for freedom threw up some great leaders who symbolised the aspirations of millions of people for economic betterment. Their weapons were strikes and civil disobedience, but managing the future called for different skills. Instead of dedicating themselves to economic development, they wasted time in democratic assemblies debating what to do with colonial statues in public squares. Educated young people became disenchanted with politics. They had neither the inclination nor the talent to appeal to the lowest common denominator that going into politics demanded. It had become a game of demagoguery, hypocrisy, and slogan mongering.

The worst manifestation of that era was the creation of the public sector which blocked billions of dollars in inefficient management. A new movement is afoot, however, to re-examine the public sector more objectively. At his impressive New Delhi office, I asked V. Krishnamurthy, chairman of the Steel Authority of India, the nation's largest corporation, whether the country really needed the public sector. 'Its predominant role in the past was to accelerate India's economic development,' he said. 'Immediately after independence, there was little infrastructure or large-scale industries. Entrepreneurs with wealth and the necessary will to take the risks involved in massive investments with long gestation periods were missing. So the public sector had an important role to play. But over a period of time the whole thing got distorted.'

Bureaucratic busybodies became the curse of sectors private and public. Civil servants even now cannot resist taking their finger out of the perk-infested pie of state control. In Krishnamurty's view, if the proper balance of interest cannot be attained, 'then I'd say government should gradually withdraw from the public sector.' Wouldn't politicians scream that India was being sold out? 'You need bold leadership to do it. I believe practical considerations are going to dictate that we should give more and more freedom to private enterprise. After all, the great quality of an Indian has always been his enterprise.' As we said goodbye, I looked out of the window at the panoramic view of the capital. Across the inviting fairways of the Delhi Golf Club lay a landscape dotted with a thousand forgotton monuments of Hindu, Muslim, and British India. I wondered whether posterity will think of independent India's industrial monuments more kindly. The ancient Brahmins controlled India's soul. The Mughals subjugated its body. The British enslaved its mind. But independent India seems to have willingly surrendered its spirit to a coterie of politicians who are loath to set it free. And that freedom of spirit will not come to India or the rest of Asia till businessmen demonstrate a sense of social responsibility. To an average citizen, the public sector is no worse than the control of business and industry by a handful of families. Our private enterprises must increasingly be managed by professional managers.

At the triennial conference of the Asian Association of Management Organisations in Hong Kong, Dr Freddie Mehta, director of Tata Industries, spoke about government's role in a mixed economy. India is paying a high price for 25 years of socialism, he said. The middle class is becoming resentful of the public sector, and the recent wave of competition has benefited all. I asked if it were not true that it is politically difficult for the government to deregulate the economy because it will be seen to offer a bonanza to private companies, most of whom are closely linked with one family or the other. He agreed that the time had come to give professional managers a larger say in running private enterprises. As long as private companies are perceived by the public to act only in their own self-interest, it will be difficult to win back control from bureaucrats.

If our business people embrace the concept of enlightened self-interest, they will be in a better position to question the monopoly of government not only in certain industrial sectors but in education, public housing, transportation, electricity, and water supplies. At the same time they should not remain silent when free enterprise threatens our way of life or destroys our natural resources. Our beaches and forests are our collective heritage. I am saddened when I hear some business people tell me that some of the social evils that irresponsible economic development is creating will go away with greater prosperity.

Take Phuket, for instance, to which thousands of tourists flock from Europe every winter. To them it is an idyllic pleasure spot. But to local residents like Somboon, it's home. Tourism has brought visible prosperity to the islanders, including Somboon and his wife. He runs a boat-rental business on the beach and she makes life-jackets at home. With a child on the way, they are extending their one-bedroom house-workshop. But progress has also brought problems. 'What happens if our baby is a girl—how can we bring her up in this town?' he asks, obviously referring to the teeming population of bar hostesses. Earlier, as we drove down 'the Strip', he had pointed to the unending row of bars, saying that for most tourists that was Phuket. He showed me that morning's lead story in a Bangkok newspaper's feature section. 'The darker side of Pattaya,' it proclaimed, 'where prostitution is a way of life.' It explored the grimness in the shadows of the plush beach hotels: 'Nart is 12 years old. Her friend, Lek, is the same age. Tonight, they are sharing the same customer, a big American sailor.' About 12 per cent of Thailand's one million prostitutes as of 1985 were children under fourteen. Somboon angrily flings the paper aside. 'It's only a matter of time,' he sighs, 'before we're worse than Pattaya.'

Corporate citizenship

Corporate citizenship is the most undervalued asset today in Asia. And yet in the rapidly changing socio-economic environment, it will be the most dynamic force for free enterprise to win its due right and respect. But it will not be won by a few hundred dollars' donation to the Red Cross or some pseudo-sponsorship of the arts. Often a narrow purpose can bring the worthy cause of corporate citizenship into disrepute. Jeremy Pickle, president of Westbig's Asian operations, once read in the newspaper about the local philharmonic orchestra's efforts to turn professional. At once, he saw in it an opportunity to impress upon his head office his stature in the local community. He tried to get several managers interested in the project. But most of them could see his personal objective and the response was lukewarm. So he resorted to subtle pressure and it did not take long for smart executives to realise that the 'voluntary' assistance was part of the job. Pickle was expecting a visit from a head office VIP who was interested in music and had even composed a minor piece. His ultimate objective was to introduce the visitor to the local dignitaries associated with the philharmonic and have the orchestra play the music composed by the VIP!

Handled with sincerity, every little effort counts. Often it is not simply a question of money, but honest intentions. Feeling strongly about disabled children, Tata Chemicals, in addition to tangible help and assistance, carries poems, drawings, and other works of these youngsters on the backs of company statements to shareholders and other corporate literature. It adds a human touch to drab statistics. The following is one such poem.

I don't want you to open the door for me
Just make it wide enough for me to get through. I know my braces
   cause you to stare
I don't like them either but they help me to walk.
I may be deaf, but I am not dumb...
So please don't call me that...
I choose to talk with my hands
I used to play football, hunt and swim...
Then I lost my legs...but I didn't lose my desire
I don't see the sunset...don't pity me...
I have never seen it.
Let me walk with you...even if it's a little slower
Let me talk with you...even if it's with my hands.
If I had three wishes, I'd wish for happiness
I'd probably wish to be whole and
I'd wish to be accepted for what I am.

11 The dilemma of the expatriate wife

Dorothy Porter rang the silver bell at the dining table for the second time. Her guests could feel she was getting impatient. Fortunately, the maid appeared with the main course within a few seconds. Everyone was visibly relieved, none more than Jaye Shagun, who worked with Ben Porter in Westbig Corporation's Asia-Pacific head office. The Porters had arrived in Asia about three months earlier, and Jaye was pleased to see how quickly they had settled into their new home—even if it meant that Peggy, the office's administrative assistant for expatriates, had to spend most of her time helping with the relocation. She had also worked hard to find a good maid. But he wondered about the bell. Had his hostess seen it in a movie? Was it her idea of how the *memsahibs* managed their households in Asia?

As the evening wore on, he could sense a similar uneasiness among his colleagues and their wives. The atmosphere was full of forced formality and contrived conversation. How much better it would have been, he thought, if Dorothy had arranged an informal buffet-type dinner. After all, the purpose of the occasion was to get to know one another. Why the starched-shirt stiffness? The custom of calling servants by ringing a bell became passé about the same time that stewards of Victorian colonialism stopped being fanned with a hand-operated *punkha*. If Dorothy had tried to cook a couple of dishes herself, even if only simple things like pizza or hamburgers, her personal hand in trying to please the guests would have conveyed more warmth than a formal meal, the arrival of which is commanded by a bell.

Superficial lives

It's so easy for wives of multinational managers in Asia to fall into the trap of superficiality. Due to a desire to help their husbands' career, they often find themselves playing strange parts or following antiquated role models. In the beginning they might feel excited by this, but in time the novelty wears off and boredom and frustration set in. They find themselves suffering, often silently, from a psychological disability which neither their husbands nor the company know about. Globalisation of business has cast their menfolk in the role of commercial warriors sent out to conquer untapped markets, but has left the role of wives undefined. The managers usually know what is required of them; the wives don't.

As their new life unfolds in Hong Kong, Tokyo, or Kuala Lumpur, the average expatriate wife faces a formidable challenge. Expatriate living standards, she quickly discovers, are higher than she was used to. She must live up to her husband's elevated status. Other wives with an earlier start have set up beautiful homes. So, with a maid to take over her old functions of cleaning, washing, and cooking, the wife devotes herself to keeping up with the Joneses, often busily decorating the home with pieces of junk that go by the name of antiques. The husband, meanwhile, is frequently away on business trips and she has to cope with domestic crises on her own. After a year's hard work the flat looks good, but new problems emerge. She has met only one or two expatriate wives whom she likes. The coffee parties given by the boss's wife are utterly tedious. The other wives' conversation dwells at times on their sacrifices—jobs given up, education under-utilised, professional qualifications unrecognised—but on the whole they stick to such mundane topics as the gifts their husbands bring back from overseas trips. At office parties, meanwhile, the wife is expected to put on a bold front. After all, the company's business is booming and there are exciting new projects.

Konrad Weis, president and CEO of Bayer USA Inc., points out that the spouse and children are left to themselves trying to adapt to a strange culture, much of the time on their own:

> We—the international managers who have just been transferred—have the easy part. It is another country, yes, but it is still our company; so we are at least here on familiar ground. But who prepares the rest of the family for the daily adventures in the new schools, strange shopping centres, or (adjustments) with the new employer of the professional spouse who followed into the foreign assignment? I guess we have to admit that in general we do not prepare the families well enough, nor do we help them enough during the first months after the transfer.

Charlene, an average wife, feels that her role as mother and wife is overshadowed by the change in her lifestyle. Betty, more modern and pragmatic, consoles her, 'You're sharing in your husband's success, after all, and you'll have to agree it beats scrubbing floors and cooking back in Middletown.' Charlene, however, is concerned about the loss in the quality of her relationships, something she finds hard to define. She talks about Jane, a sensitive woman married to a burly, overbearing manager who is disliked by local employees. Jane, therefore, has been unable to befriend their wives and has taken to drinking. 'David knows what's happening to her, but is doing nothing about it.' Charlene also mentions Mabel, who has become rather neurotic, calling her 20–year old son at college every day, while people in the company callously joke about it. Elizabeth's teenage daughter is going out with an Asian boy. 'I know he's nice, but what happens when they have to separate?' Charlene is not sure whether the advantages of an international life and her husband's career prospects are adequate compensation for all the complications they have raised.

Surrounded by such doubts, some wives begin to live a life of make-believe, actively assisted by their husbands; they indulge in fantasies of social status and family background. My friend Jambon once told me about the annoying habit of his boss's wife of trying to impress people with her pedigree. 'She is so phoney,' he exclaimed. 'Her mother is visiting her and gave her an antique table probably bought on sale in some back-street shop. Last night at a dinner party at her home, the guests had to sit there all evening and listen to her tell how the wretched thing had been in her family for three generations.' Jambon added, with a pained expression, 'There are several people in the company who know that her father was a baker. What's the point in pretending he was a banker?' I could sympathise with Jambon. It reminded me of an evening of sheer torture I once spent at the house of some casual friends. I had met Joe Howley and his wife Mary when they lived in New York. Joe was now a senior manager for his company in Asia. He had bought Mary a cheap mink coat from a manufacturer's outlet. Wearing this coat at her own party, she gave the guests a tour of her house. She took pains to point out a couple of artifacts as being antiques of great value and a grandfather clock which she claimed had been in the family for over a century. As I had known Joe and Mary in New York at a time when they bought most of their clothes and furniture from cut-rate stores in Brooklyn, I found the commentary ludicrous. Unfortunately, it was hardly a unique experience. At other parties, guests are regularly forced-fed discourses on Indonesian colonial lamps, Chinese snuff bottles, Korean chests, and imitation Persian carpets.

Such cravings for attention are symptoms of the neglect from which most corporate wives suffer. They want to convince themselves and everybody else they are making the most of their husbands' overseas assignments. They want their contributions to be recognised. At a seminar in cross-cultural sensitivity for expatriate wives organised by the Asian head office of a multinational company, senior managers were astounded at the pent-up feeling of their wives against the company. The women poured out their mournful complaints about being ignored. They felt strongly that the company valued the work of their husbands but cared little about the support of the wives. Yet it is the quality of that support that quite often determines whether an overseas assignment will be a success or a failure.

Expatriate wives also suffer, though indirectly, from the status of women in Asian societies. Despite big strides made by a great number, most Asian women still exist in a social limbo. Their relationship with men is by no means on an equal footing. Professional advances notwithstanding, their most cherished quality is still supposed to be the subtle support and stability they provide to their husbands and their children. To an outsider it simply looks like male chauvinism. I once sat through a dinner at which an Australian manager lectured a Japanese colleague about women's liberation. No Australian woman, he said, would put up with the superior attitude of Japanese men. As their wives listened, the Japanese explained patiently that the relationship should not be viewed superficially. His wife may not contradict him in public, but that didn't mean she had no say in private on important matters: she managed the family's finances, took full responsibility for the children's education, and had a deep influence as a wife and mother. That, he added, was the strength of Japanese society. But the Australian was unconvinced. 'You won't know what hit you when feminism catches on in Japan,' he declared.

Loneliness

Another problem faced by expatriate wives is loneliness, caused by the twin barriers of organisational hierarchy and social and cultural differences. Managers in structured organisations tend to equate promotion with power and this naturally distances them from their colleagues. It is a wilful act of managerial masochism practised collectively to preserve corporate sanctity. The wives suffer from this practice the most as it makes personal relationships, already difficult due to cultural differences, even more complex. Often it seems that modern expatriate families—thousands of miles from home, thrust into alien cultures, deprived of familiar support systems, banished to three or four years' solitary confinement—are socially no better off than in the nineteenth century.

By far the greatest challenge, however, comes from practices which wives see as risks to their marriage—frequent travel by husbands to cities notorious for their sleazy nightlife and too many nights out with the boys on the pretext of business entertainment. The situation is aggravated by the wives' perception of Asian societies as being less severe in demanding total fidelity from the married man. No doubt the attitude in Asia to philandering males tends to be more tolerant as long as the immensely important family obligations are not neglected. These wives talk to other women about their fears and end up less than reassured. 'Let's face it,' says an English woman who has lived in Asia for a long time, 'It's the humiliation and hurt to one's pride that's difficult to bear, though I must confess that after so many years in Asia I feel Western women are brought up to think about marriage unrealistically. In the end it doesn't really matter as long as he keeps quiet about it.'

A Chinese woman thinks Asian wives see casual infidelities on the part of a husband as far less of a personal affront, though feelings, of course, are hurt. But to most expatriate wives, marriage is a personal relationship that is drastically changed if either partner suspects the other of being unfaithful. In this context, a helpful Asian secretary can sometimes unwittingly pose a problem. Margaret, for example, didn't mind helping to supervise a few changes her new boss wanted in his flat before his family joined him. But his wife, when she arrived, was most unhappy. Margaret got the impression that the wrongly placed electrical outlets and other minor things were all her fault. The manager could easily sense his wife's jealousy. It had been his first experience with an Asian secretary and he had been delighted with her courtesy and cooperation, not to mention the coffee served dutifully at his desk three times a day. But he began to rely on Margaret for so many personal and domestic chores that it was easy for his wife to misunderstand the relationship.

Asian expatriate wives

Asian expatriate wives fare marginally better, but they too face a number of problems. The international lifestyle that comes with a position in a foreign company can impose social strains. Wives usually have to participate in company functions. But many do not speak good English, are shy with strangers, do not drink, and find it difficult to make small talk. This can create a tension between the manager's working life and his home life. Their children, with a foreign education, tend to aspire to bigger breaks in life. The family's aim may become focused on sending the eldest to Oxbridge or an Ivy League college. But this pride is soon tempered by the realisation that the child is becoming alienated from the old ways and customs. Home on vacation, Sunita doesn't fold her hands properly to greet visitors. Murad spends evenings at a fashionable disco. These things hurt and horrify proud Asian parents.

As Asia modernises itself, professional managers, at the forefront of change, are both its primary beneficiaries and its victims. Through management techniques, travel, and meeting foreign businessmen, they become internationalised. Yet this involves a degree of suppression of their cultural identities. So they want all the more to be Chinese, Indian, Malay, or Thai at home. This creates problems as far as wives are concerned. They are expected to be both modern and traditional. The company functions or cocktail parties become charged with strain. If they wear a kimono or a sari and stand around holding a glass of orange juice, they are treated to patronising conversation. 'If we smoke and drink and wear a skirt, we may be treated as equals,' says a Thai manager's wife, 'but we feel an undercurrent of hostility from other Asian women.' To be sociable they may drink, but then they risk being considered too forward, betrayers of the standards of Asian womanhood.

Traditional values

In Asia, the strength of traditional family values makes the position of a modern corporate wife far more complicated than that of their counterparts in the West. The case of Leslie Koh throws some light on the dilemma in which many young modern couples are caught. Koh graduated from an Australian university and joined the Singapore branch of a multinational bank. In the last twenty years, he has risen to one of the top jobs held by a local employee. About fifteen years ago he married the daughter of a wealthy merchant. She manages part of her father's business. Between them they own a large house, a spacious town apartment, and two cars. Koh, one of four children, was brought up in a very poor but closely-knit family. What the children lacked in food and clothing was more than made up for with generous love from their mother. Koh married his wife because she had the warmth and simple nature like his mother. At home he expects her to be a typical old-fashioned mum, but outside he wants her to be a modern woman. He would like her to share more of his busy social life, particularly in entertaining visitors from the bank's head office in the USA. He is envious of a colleague—with whom he is in direct competition for the next promotion—because his wife is a very good hostess and has all the social graces. At the same time Koh hates the idea that his wife should have to play a social game. He would prefer to see her as a devoted mother to their two children. In private, he confides that he is unhappy and wonders whether all the hard work in building a career has been worth it. He is not sure whether he unconsciously strove for more money in life, but he knows that something which was precious in his parents' home is missing from his own.

Sometime ago *World Executive's Digest* published the results of a survey on the views of managers on spouses' contribution. Dual-career marriages, it said, are more common in Asia than one would surmise.

> Fully 65.9% of the spouses of the managers surveyed work full-time, most of them as professionals or office workers or managers. When asked what their spouses' most important contribution would be to business success, the Asian managers say it is the ability to maintain a satisfying and well-run home. This is in contrast to American managers, who consider their spouses' emotional support most important.

Of course, contemporary families are in transition in Asia. Professor Meguro Yoriko of Sophia University calls it a process of individualisation:

> Changing women's roles and self-perception are probably the most powerful factors forcing family life to change, and the direction of change will be towards greater individual orientation. Because of this change, which has been going on for at least a few decades in the USA and for perhaps a decade or so in Japan, the major function of the family is now considered as being to satisfy the emotional and expressive needs of family members more than other types of needs. If you ask sociologists in the USA what the family function is, they will say it is to meet expressive needs, not necessarily to give family members financial support or social status, which used to be the major family functions. The definition of the family has thus changed.

Meanwhile companies must do more to provide cultural orientation to expatriate spouses. Unfortunately there is insufficient realisation of domestic strife and unhappiness resulting from failure to adjust to a new environment. The reward these days of working abroad is no longer the long-awaited return to the home country with a pot of gold; it is in living and sharing the present with others. Failures can't be explained away by management as the inability of individuals to cope with change. That's a short-sighted approach, based on the outdated excuse that the private lives of employees are no concern of the company.

12 Asian women managers

Though successful professionally, women managers seem to face many of the same cultural and family constraints as do corporate wives. A profile of Asian women managers shows that though they can be as tough as they come, they can't completely shake off the feeling that their real place is at home. They are prepared to forego love, marriage, and motherhood to win the battle of the boardroom. They aspire to prove themselves not just as equal but even superior to men—but the price of success worries them. Eighteen top executives among them go public for the first time in baring their souls to a team of women researchers in *Corporate Women Managers in Southeast Asia*, published by the Asian Institute of Management. It not only documents the successful assault on male-dominated executive suites, but reveals trade-offs along the way. The new denizens of the business world are brave but sorely bruised. They entered the rat race not to make a living but to feel worthier as human beings and more interesting to men. Sadly, many think they have lost something precious in the bargain. Some feel that they have ceased functioning as women. Others are saddled with agonising guilt.

Says Jannie Tay, managing director of Singapore's No. 1 watch-retailing chain, 'In this society, women have to work twice as hard as men to be thought half as good. After all, we still live and work in an environment which is predominantly controlled by men.' Seen by her staff as pushy but also warm and sensitive, Tay would have preferred to remain a teacher. Family exigencies forced her into business. One of her daughters was born with severe brain damage and died nine years later. Another had a congenital handicap also. Tay is prouder of what she achieved in struggling to help the children than she is with success in business. But fighting the battle of life on two fronts left its scars. She found comfort in the Indian guru Sai Baba, whose spiritual teachings 'led me to greater compassion, patience, tolerance, and understanding of people.'

Salinee, vice-president of an American bank in Bangkok, observes that women first have to overcome prejudice about their abilities just to gain basic acceptance. They are blamed for being too picky about petty things. She advises women managers to be *ohn-wan* (sweet) but not *ohn-eh* (weak). Salinee often gets home well past the dinner hour. By then her husband and son have both eaten a meal cooked by the maid—certainly not the quality Salinee would fix for her spouse. 'If I were home before dinner time, I could prepare food for him, have the table set nicely,' she sighs. 'I could, let's say, take off his shoes, give him his slippers. I could bring him a warm towel or a cold towel to wipe his face.'

Says Sharifah Kassim, personnel manager of a leading Malaysian engineering firm: 'Malaysian men are not used to working with women. They treat them the way they treat their wives at home. That's where the trouble begins.' She is grateful for her husband's understanding about her job but regrets that her family has taken second place. Aida Gonzales Gordon, president of a Philippine garment-making company, also believes women have to choose between home and career. She has yet to meet a woman, Gordon says, who can look her 'straight in the eye' and claim 'excellence in both'. She herself always knew work came first. Others aren't too sure. Their heart is either still in the home or heavy with remorse about missed chances. Carol Koh, resident manager of Singapore's Orchard Hotel, says her early career lost her a fiancé. She became so concerned with 'superficial' etiquette that she demanded from him perfect social manners. She now finds sustenance in Christianity.

Half-way to modernism

Ivy Goh, whom I met a couple of years ago, is a modern young manager and a modern young woman. She is in charge of marketing at the Singapore subsidiary of Tai Ping Carpets. Career advancement, she says, offers a sense of achievement and independence. It also separates her from millions of other Asian women who sacrifice jobs for marriage. There's a lot more to life than marriage, says Goh, who speaks proudly of her mother's ambition for her: 'She didn't want me to be just another woman.' Ivy Goh drives a Porsche. She goes to fashionable discos and dresses with flair. Her lifestyle, she believes, is something she has earned. But to out-of-town buyers, it often suggests possibilities beyond orders for carpets. Such misunderstandings don't upset her. She merely points to the college degree on her card. At work she is a competent supervisor. But as a female, in what she calls a 'transient world half-way to modernism', she has to be watchful of the male ego. Sometimes she reprimands subordinates indirectly through other male employees. When critical of one she may praise another to show she is not being hard on men. She knows their pride can be easily hurt. She has to be careful about going out for drinks or meals with them. 'Feelings get involved so easily,' she says. 'I want them to treat me only as a colleague.'

Ivy Goh is part of an elite group of female managers. In Bangladesh and Indonesia not one manager in a hundred is a woman, while in the USA 37 per cent of corporate managers are women. Asian working women are normally not free to decide whether they want to marry and have children. Marriage is expected of them, even if they are pursuing full-time careers. Most Asian women in business are from relatively well-off families; work is more a symbol of freedom than a matter of necessity. Life and values remain centred on the home. They do not feel Ivy Goh's strong need to compete. Is it really necessary to embrace total modernism to be the equal of men at work? Does a woman have to renounce marriage or, even more difficult, manage without stress both a career and motherhood? Does she have to look slim and elegant like the working women in TV commercials? Modern professional women who think like that have been grievously misled. What about the bald, boring, self-opinionated, pot-bellied, belching men on the top of the corporate ladder? Who are they to set such blatantly unfair standards for women managers? On the contrary, most Asian men, if they have to work for a woman, would prefer someone who embodies the deeper Asian ideals of understanding, forbearance, fairness, and patience.

A boss in cheongsam

Though women in Asian societies may be depressed in status, they are not oppressed. They enjoy an almost matriarchal status at home, partly through custom and partly through subtle manipulation. Many successful Asian men ascribe their achievements to the selfless dedication of their mothers in strengthening the family. The qualities needed for that are venerated everywhere in Asia. Asian women managers should employ those qualities to their advantage at work rather than try to compete on modern terms. My old friend Robert Yeo told me in Singapore about the late Dr Ruth Wong, who used to be head of the Institute of Education where he teaches. She was a wonderful administrator, he says, kind and efficient—and always impressive in her cheongsam. Four Asian countries have produced women heads of government. Though modern and progressive, none felt any need to abrogate her past.

Multinationals can play an imporant role in developing women managers able to combine the best of Asian and Western cultures. Misplaced sensitivity in some of these firms has led to an assumption that Asian men will not accept female managers. In fact, they will be only too willing to give support and loyalty to women who bring the virtues of home and family to the increasingly amoral world of modern business.

Asian women managers should ignore such gratuitous advice as Juli Weber's in her book *Better Business Images and Etiquette*. 'Ruffles and frills tend to make you look feminine, which to employers means weak. A bow, modest ruffle or jabot at the neckline of a silk shirt is best suited to senior-level women who have worked their way up,' she pronounces. 'Senior-level women in Europe and North America are finding more freedom in business attire now they are no longer a rare breed. However, that's not true in Asia. Conservatism is still the order of the day.' One is left wondering whether Ms Weber considers cheongsam or sari conservative or frilly attire.

A distinct advantage women have over men in business is their softer approach to leadership, says Robert Waterman. 'They have a lot fewer hangups about being the kind of boss that I claim brings out the best in productivity. The problem is, women have mixed emotions about that,' he says. 'They've got a natural advantage, but the role models they're surrounded with are the other kind. So they feel they must suppress what's natural for them and be the tough guy.'

The art of gentle management

More and more Asian women managers are, however, discovering that their inherent feminine qualities can be a help rather than a hindrance in business. They are the practitioners of the gentle art of management. Cory de la Paz, senior partner of Price Waterhouse in Manila, insists on getting hard work from her hundreds of dedicated employees, but also finds it hard to hide compassion. She knows her people work longer hours than those in other organisations. 'I find it difficult to accept, but it is happening,' she says. 'Our women auditors, for example, have to work till three or four in the morning. Some are even pregnant. I have told them that they cannot choose the job they will be assigned to. If they want equal pay for equal work, they just have to do the job.' Her search for a happy compromise, a gentle but firm way of handling things, extends to her family. She feels children nowadays are different because parents have more money. If you shower material luxuries on them at a very young age, their values are destroyed. 'Sometimes I feel our daughter is very materialistic, very conscious of the latest things. If someone has a computer, she must have one too.' But Cory is not the type to give in easily. 'Sometimes my daughter says, "How come you can't buy that for me when I know you have the money?" I say, "I may have the money but it's still not right for you to get it. You have to do with less. Only then will you be able to develop better values." ' Then, echoing the ambivalence of other well-off working parents, she adds that she doesn't know how a 10–year old child accepts such pre-scripts. But she smiles warmly, and allows herself a few moments to reminisce about old values—principles acquired from rural upbring-ing in which a lot of playmates and climbing trees were more fun than staying in your room and playing with a robot.

Since the family has been such a dominating influence in their lives, Asian women managers will be unwilling to abdicate their role as mothers and wives in the foreseeable future. As managers they would succeed by being themselves rather than men in dresses. They are unlikely to blindly follow their more aggressive Western counter-parts. Take someone like Anne Brzenk. She works for a smallish private company in San Francisco where, in addition to her duties as a supervisor, she has been put in charge of 'international development'. It was in this capacity that she met my entrepreneur friend Sam Lau from Hong Kong. Sam wanted to discuss the possibility of introduc-ing one of her company's products to Asia. He found her most unpleasant to deal with. She was trying so hard to be like a tough guy, he told me. She was too visibly affected by the success syn-drome. She seemed to believe that if she rushed she would get to the end of the rainbow sooner. Sam likes to deal with people in a relaxed way and found her brisk and 'efficient' manner a poor cloak for inexperience in international business. Anne Brzenk's company did not get Sam Lau's order.

Expatriate women managers are often upset at their Asian coun-terparts showing deference to men and staying in the background. Swiss-born Christine Cereghetti, in charge of public relations for foreign guests at Seoul's Lotte Hotel found the second-class status of women difficult to accept. 'When I first arrived here,' she says 'I just couldn't absorb the cultural shock, and I still don't understand the depth of sexual discrimination that women have to endure in Korea.' Cereghetti describes an incident that made a particularly big impress-ion on her. A woman with whom she worked, and who spoke English very well, was asked to translate a Korean document into English while her male colleagues looked on. The woman refused, claiming she could not perform the task. Cereghetti, however, knew she could do the job easily and later asked why she had refused. The woman told her that if she had done the job, it would have embar-rassed her male colleagues and damaged their pride.

But Sato Kumi, president of Cosmo Public Relations Corporation in Tokyo, counsels Western women working in Japan to pay close attention to the customs and traditions of the country and of the company they are working for. 'They should not try to fight battles over such things as Japanese female employees serving tea to the men in the office. An outsider is not likely to change such a custom and it would only generate bad feelings in the office.' Women managers have a long way to go in creating a greater awareness of their growing contribution to the economic development of Asia. Sato's advice is sound that success is unlikely to be achieved by women liberators taking up issues such as making tea. There are scores of other areas which need intelligent discussion and review by management. Are employers serious about hiring more women managers and developing their skills? If so, they must introduce special training programs to help them adjust to what is still a man's world. Asian women themselves must determine how far they want to go and how to achieve the right balance between love and devotion to children and corporate success.

13 Embarking on an Asian assignment

An understanding of how other people perceive us is the first step towards establishing a successful relationship with them. Therefore, a manager starting an assignment in Asia must have some idea of what local employees collectively think of expatriates. I posed this question to a group of Asian middle managers at a recent seminar. Their responses reflect not only old views but also changing expectations. Professional competence, for instance, which in the past was often singled out as a particularly desirable quality in expatriates, is now taken for granted. A greater value is placed these days not merely on a person's skill, but on *how* they impart that skill to others. Overall, the responses provide a helpful insight into how expatriates are regarded by Asian managers.

Traits and qualities in expatriate managers

First, expatriate managers are considered to be fair in their dealings. Most Asian middle managers rate them high on that score. They believe that expatriates find it easier to be objective because they are emotionally detached. Of course, some do have strong personal likes and dislikes, but as a rule they base their decisions on hard facts. Second, they are quite liberal: less picky about behaviour and more patient with aggressive individualistic traits. 'As long as you do your job well, your personal conduct does not matter a great deal,' explains one manager. Third, expatriate managers are looked upon as fairly generous: they are unlikely to go over an expense statement with a fine-tooth comb, and are sympathetic when someone is caught in a temporary financial difficulty. Fourth, they are frank and straightforward: open about things they approve or disapprove of without unduly hiding their feelings.

On the negative side, expatriate managers are seen to be excessively career-oriented. They look at their overseas stint simply as a stepping stone to the next level of the corporate hierarchy.

131

They spend an inordinate time reporting to head office and trying to make visiting top brass happy. Second, their cultural assimilation is superficial, but they tend to boast about their knowledge of local customs and complex political matters. They give much credence to what they learn from friends at the club or close circle of business associates. Third, they are not trained in transferring skills and are given to imparting professional expertise in fits and starts. Fourth, they go by first impressions in forming an opinion about the career potential of subordinates. Appearance, accent, and demeanour play a more important part in deciding them than real ability.

A few other impressions—considered neither good nor bad—complete the picture. Expatriates spend too much time in decorating their homes. A few may be genuinely interested in local arts and crafts, but most use these objects for mere display. They appear to be bound by a vague foreign community convention that makes them conform to a socially acceptable standard. They mix mostly with others of their own nationality, though their children now make more local friends. They are fond of talking about their maids. Their reading consists of paperbacks depicting a romantic and fictional-ised account of Asia's past. They often use these books as a guide to local history. They are keen on sports, both watching and play-ing, and share a deep-rooted communal urge to remain loyal to a particular sport or a team to demonstrate a continued sense of belonging.

Not long after the seminar, I heard a British radio program which consisted of reminiscences of officials and businessmen who lived in colonial Malaysia 40 years ago. Their recurring themes were cricket, clubs, clothes, drinks, and dinner parties. There was emphasis on the exclusion of Malays, Chinese, and Indians from expatriate social life. There was nothing which provided any meaningful insight into the political, economic, or spiritual lives of the people in those times. Of course, there is much more broad-based integration today and a shift away from the narrow focus on expatriate lifestyles, especially by younger managers. Yet the old tales of pink gins on the veranda and dry martinis at the club persist.

Despite these lingering images, both sides are aware of the real benefits which each brings to the party. These can be summed up as the 'Five Cs' of Asian managers (including Asian expatriate managers) and the 'Five Es' of Western expatriates. First of all, Asians bring with them a continuity, a sense of history, a feeling of the context in which the company is working in Asia. Second, they have a natural commitment to the region and to its economic growth and wellbeing. Third, Asian managers have an inborn cultural sensitivity. Fourth, they bring valuable connections. Fifth, they know how to use com-passion which is perhaps the best word to describe the quality needed to balance the ever-growing power that managers acquire as they rise through a corporation.

The first contribution of expatriate managers is expertise. Second, they bring ethos: exposure at head office to the workings, values, and perspective of the corporation. Third, they are often able to provide endorsement for Asian colleagues and their ideas. Schemes and brainwaves that might otherwise have been ignored are encouraged and exploited. Fourth is their eagerness and pioneering spirit. Lastly, they help with esprit de corps, encouraging employees to put the aims of the company above their private ambitions.

Cultural differences between Asian and Western management

These qualities add up to a formidable list. But they can be ineffective in the absence of mutual respect and cultural sensitivity. Many global managers do not realise they are walking into a cultural minefield when they enter Asia, and are oblivious to the profound damage their unintentional insensitivity can cause. In *Getting your Yen's Worth: How to Negotiate with Japan, Inc.*, Bob Moran points to several differences between Americans and Japanese. To a large extent, they also apply to most other Asian societies. In Japan, a manager rarely displays knowledge and, in fact, may even underplay his understanding. American negotiators, on the other hand, take pride in tackling problems single-handedly, in demonstrating that they know the pertinent facts, and in being able to address any issue concerning the subject at hand. In Japan there is less eye contact and more silence during negotiations than in the West. The Japanese have a great deal less compulsion to formulate instant judgments and answers. They will often pause for a moment before commenting or answering, considering carefully what has been said.

During a negotiating session, most English-speaking businessmen understandably address their remarks to the person with the best command of their language. Moran warns, however, that this not only embarrasses the translator but may also offend the other members of the negotiating team. He further notes that it is regarded as very rude to interrupt an authority figure. The Japanese believe that Americans have a habit of passing very quickly over the areas of agreement and giving a high emphasis to disagreement. In fact, he argues, they talk about little else, as if that were the most important subject. The Japanese negotiators, on the other hand, spend a lot of time reviewing areas of agreement. Moran therefore advises Americans to 'return to areas of agreement as this will build a strong relationship'.

It is also most important *how* disagreements are phrased. I know of an Australian manager who was admired back home for his blunt and forthright manner. Soon after his transfer to Hong Kong, he was involved in some price negotiations in China. He told a Chinese official in Guangzhou to his face that he was lying about the lower price of plastics from a competitive source. Two horrified Hong Kong Chinese employees who were present later told top management that that one sentence had wiped out months of hard work.

Sometime ago I had a stimulating chat in Melbourne with Geoff Allen, the articulate executive director of the Business Council of Australia. He told me frankly: 'One of the myths we've developed is that Asian countries really like Australian straightforwardness. With the Australian manager it's all out on the table. He doesn't have a hidden agenda—though I'm not denying his bluntness and even the crass aggression. We've been led to believe that our directness is appreciated.' But the long-established Australian residents of Asia are the first to point out that it takes time to build relationships. What the Australian thinks is 'open and frank' is quite likely to be seen as impolite and offensive in Asia.

In Beijing, Wang Ming has seen foreigners committing deplorable faux pas. She studied business administration at an American university and returned to take a job in the office of a large foreign company. One company, she says, sent out letters to high-ranking officials asking them to meet their visiting president at his hotel. 'That would have been a breach of protocol even in Washington,' she observes. On another occasion a cocktail reception was being given for the company's chief executive. An important guest remarked that Wang had been most persistent in urging him to attend. 'He meant it as a compliment. He was saying I was conscientious and respectful,' she said. But the visitor, totally misconstruing the remark, later reproached her for 'forcing' people to attend. Wang's Beijing's boss is an expatriate. She says he has no respect for, or loyalty to, his own staff. She wonders why companies bother to assign to China expatriate who take so long to understand the country when there are so many Chinese in the USA who could be employed after being trained in business. Furthermore, 'Why don't they make use of China's vast human resources?' she asks, not a little impatiently. 'In our office the best treatment is reserved for the expatriates, followed by the ABCs (American-born Chinese), then the Hong Kong Chinese, and finally poor me.' Wang Ming, a pleasant, intelligent, and articulate woman, resents her employer treating her as just 'one of the billion Chinese'.

Unfortunately, a lot of newcomers take their cue from 'old hands'—mostly British companies who are living in the past. These companies continue to manage their affairs as if nothing has changed.

They cling tenaciously to a bygone organisational structure, with its patronising attitudes and long lunches at predominantly British clubs. 'Twenty-five years of independence here,' observes a Singaporean manager, 'has made no difference to the way they live and do business.' They seem old-fashioned even to the young British managers they employ. One new Cambridge graduate calls them 'anachronistic in so many ways'.

Towards the end of 1985 I met Chin Teck Huat, then general manager of Cold Storage Holdings, a big Singapore food wholesaler founded in 1903 and controlled by the family of the Earl of Portarlington, who lives in Sydney. (In 1987 the company was taken over by the Wattie group of New Zealand.) At the time, Chin was most unhappy with his job (he left not long afterwards to become CEO of Intraco, a large government-controlled, public listed trading company). He told me there was very little consultation at Cold Storage. People were told what management thought was necessary and heard about it just before action was supposed to be carried out. 'I find this job strange, to say the least,' he said. 'Management-wise, they are very expat-orientated.' Decisions are taken mainly by expatriate managers and everybody is expected to get on with it. Cultural differences are not taken into account. If your immediate superior thinks you're great, you're great, and if he thinks you're lousy, you're lousy.'

I met Gerald Minjoot, a director of Inchcape (headed by another earl) in Singapore, at about the same time. He was more sanguine about management in the old colonial conglomerate. The London head office, he explained, is an investor in the classical sense—interested in cash flow, returns, and strategic planning. Personnel, pricing, and marketing are left to local companies. As long as targets are met, problems are few. Head office visitors are primarily 'sector directors', interested in the financial picture. Minjoot conceded that its management development is weak. 'I've had to fight for most of the formal training and career movement I've had myself, but this is changing. We've just established a training centre and run our first year's program for key executives. So we're in transition, but we don't do enough yet, in my opinion.' In Hong Kong I phoned an Inchcape subsidiary to ask for a brochure. The woman I spoke to told me she couldn't send it right away because the company mail went out only every other day. Awed by an explanation reminiscent of mail clippers sailing on designated days, I persevered, 'Why not every day?' 'Because that's not company policy,' was the reply. In big advertisements in the local papers, the company had announced special terms for a certain product. When I made my enquiry, I was told to wait a week as it was necessary to get head office approval to offer the terms advertised.

Ten tips for the new expatriate manager

Living obdurately in the past can be addictive and hazardous to survival. Asia is changing every day and successful managers recognise the need to adapt rapidly. Newcomers must be particularly alert to the expectations modern Asian managers have of them. Here's my list of ten tips on how to successfully launch yourself as an international manager in Asia.

1 Build an early consensus

Soon after your assignment, pick a senior Asian in the office who, by reason of personality or job duties, will be fairly frank with their views. Make it a point to seek this confidant's opinions not only in business matters, but also in aspects relating to the whole gamut of social behaviour, including those you might feel quite assured about. Don't wait too long before establishing a rapport with your new co-workers. Get all the employees under you together *informally* over *dim sum* or *makan kecil* to talk about broad issues (sharing of food together is an important ritual). Follow it up with buffet lunches in smaller groups for the people who directly report to you. Invite all of them to have a say, about anything on their minds. Don't act like an ambassador from the head office. Don't put your strategy on the table too early, even if to you it appears self-evident; such grand visions should be outlined much later. Keep up the dialogue, even if you feel that recurrent debating points have been exhausted. Convince employees that you sincerely want to maintain a dialogue with them. Don't announce promotions, firings, organisational changes, or new policies in the first two or three months. They would be seen by Asian managers as too impetuous, brash, and egotistical. As far as possible, make such decisions by way of consensus so that none is viewed as arbitrary. Most importantly, praise often and generously every action or thing you find praiseworthy. Don't be afraid that a pat on the back of a subordinate who is not a top performer will compromise your high standards. Don't use recognition as a goal to competitiveness. Use it visibly as a promoter of harmony. Be a team leader.

2 Renounce stereotypes

The tendency to stereotype by race is almost universal. On the surface it may seem harmless, but very often racial stereotypes develop into prejudices. Descriptions such as inscrutable, devious, and corrupt are unfortunate legacies of the past when the West considered itself morally superior to Asia. People don't 'jabber' in foreign languages, and not all Japanese 'suck air through their teeth'. New-comers to Asia can easily acquire misleading notions. Within a few days they may hear about argumentative Indians, easygoing Filipinos, chauvinistic Singaporeans, timid Thais, laid-back Malays, venal Indonesians, and inscrutable Chinese. They may be told by someone with perhaps one year's longer acquaintance with the region that Chinese and Malays don't get along together, that Indians and Pakistanis harbour mutual animosity, and that the Japanese are not accepted in Southeast Asia because people still remember the occupa-tion of their countries during the war. These are stereotype percep-tions inherited from the past and are based on a passive, subterranean, and lingering prejudice. Asians are quick to feel it—so be careful in taking early steps to actively shake off these perceptions.

3   Make friends early

It's easier to make friends when you are a new arrival. If you leave it too long, people begin to think you are not interested. I have talked with a number of managers who worked in Asia for many years and are now retired in their home countries. All of them, without excep-tion, rate their friendship with colleagues and others as the most memorable experience of their overseas assignments. Looking back, some regret that they did not try harder to develop a larger circle of friends.

Sadly, some managers don't realise that they have no friends until it is too late. I once spent an entire afternoon at the magnificent home of the expatriate head of an Asian subsidiary hearing how lonely it is to be Number One. His remedy? Classical music played at a deafen-ing volume. It was the saddest version of Mozart's 'Musical Joke' I have ever heard. 'We have lived in Singapore for three years and have only once been invited to a local home,' a European manager told me. He did not realise that he had not made any effort himself to make close friends and that the people he did know only saw him within the context of the corporate hierarchy.

4   Be a multicultural host

If you are hosting an office party, don't plan it like a board meeting. There is plenty of opportunity during office-hour meetings to posi-tion people according to job level. In the evenings, emphasise the social aspect and arrange seating to make for lively conversation. Try to encourage employees of different nationalities to mix. I recall an evening river cruise in Bangkok at which expatriate managers took up one side of the boat and Thai employees the other. There was a lot of drinking, the band played old Western favourites, and the affair turned into a private party for the expatriates. The Thais felt left out and were thoroughly dispirited. Remember that informal parties are much more fun. A Malay manager told me of a dinner his new boss's wife arranged at home for visiting executives, obviously to impress them. Only a few local couples were invited. The best china was displayed and the maids served the drinks in crystal glasses. One of them made a mistake in the table setting and was instantly chided by the hostess. 'It's impossible to train servants in Malaysia!' she complained. Nobody enjoyed the party. A less formal affair with a balanced mixture of nationalities would have been better. The visitors, subjected to so much formal business entertainment, would perhaps have preferred a relaxed evening with Asian food and entertainment.

Don't be inhibited about conversation. Most expatriates, following Western etiquette, won't talk about religion or politics at social gatherings. But Asians don't observe such taboos. So these occasions can provide opportunities for visitors to learn about cultures, customs, politics, and current events, turning the evening—provided employees know they can speak freely—into a stimulating experience. Don't limit your view of an employee to the narrow framework of their job. Scratch under the surface—and in an Asian manager you will find a politician, a preacher. At these social events, don't treat an employee as only an employee, a manager as only a manager, but rather as the interesting, talented people they really are. Reverend Lee Ching Chee of the Church of Christ in China says, 'One of the major differences between Chinese and Westerners is that the Westerner thinks of what we *do*, whereas the Chinese thinks of what we *are*.'

Be sensitive to food restrictions. Hindus don't eat beef and Muslims don't eat pork. Also, it's best not to have too long a cocktail hour before serving dinner. Drinking is not part of Asian social life to the same extent that it is in the West. Many Asians are not comfortable with drinking, especially when their wives are present. After a few drinks they tend to get emotional and more easily excited than Western colleagues. People who don't drink find it tedious to wait too long. Even if you are celebrating something, don't serve only champagne. You must give your guests a choice. Your Asian guests may not stay very long after the meal is over. Don't be offended—it is not usually the custom to linger on for hours over brandy and liqueurs.

5 Look for latent disagreements

Early in your new assignment you must quickly familiarise yourself with your department's immediate past. You are unlikely to face open disagreement or hostility, but a 'latent disagreement' from the past can quite often kill your projects. For example, not long ago I met Jim Sharp, an expatriate manager who felt totally defeated in trying to get his viewpoint understood by one of his key Asian colleagues. After three months at his company's Asian office, Jim had developed a new business plan he believed would boost profitability. It focused on concentrating manpower, money, and management time on certain countries and downgrading, for the time being, efforts to develop other markets where the company had experienced setbacks. 'But I've failed to convince Vincent,' he told me sadly. 'I'm afraid he simply doesn't think the way I do.' After some discussion it became clear that Jim had unknowingly inherited a latent disagreement between expatriate and Asian managers in his company. Those sent out from head office invariably pushed for immediate growth in profits, while the Asians usually felt the company should exploit opportunities to build future business. Obviously, in Jim's plan, Vincent saw a recurrence of the old pattern. He had worked with many expatriate managers who had limited their horizons to a two- or three-year assignment. It was easy to see why Jim's 'strategic planning' appeared suspect to Vincent. Because he had not analysed the problem at this level, Jim was unaware of the latent disagreement threatening his plan. His company, without realising it, had let disagreement become institutionalised. Its Asian managers were left without a sense of identity with the company's purpose.

To remedy such a situation you must give your associates a broader role in the debate about the company's future. You must encourage prolonged discussion to give them a feeling of belonging. Gradually they will begin to feel that the company does not look upon them merely as implementers of a policy that dovetails nicely with the career aspirations of migrant managers. Once plans are thrashed out openly, mature managers can live with differences of opinion.

6 Respect religion, not superstition

One of the first things an Old Asia Hand will point out to new expatriate managers is the strength of superstitions in Asia. More years have gone by than Donald Chesworth cares to remember since he was first assigned to Asia, but his story relates to a time when he had been at his job only a few weeks. He was delighted with his Chinese secretary, a modern, widely-travelled young lady. Chesworth took her to lunch one day hoping for a pleasant interlude in his busy settling-down period. Instead, he had to listen to a fanatical monologue about *fung shui*. She earnestly advised him to have a geomancer survey his office without delay. Dreadful things happen to those who don't pay heed. One fellow died of a heart attack sitting in his office chair; another had a stroke.

Every foreign manager in Asia encounters superstition sooner or later. But what, in the no-nonsense world of business, is a manager to make of it? To denounce beliefs as primitive is not likely to be helpful. However, it is certainly not necessary to follow local superstitions to appease employees. Modern managers should by all means try to help junior colleagues acquire a rational understanding of cause and effect. In fact, in my experience, most of the expatriate managers who adopt Asian superstitions tend to be insensitive to the more important aspects of national cultures. Having office furniture moved around by a *fung shui* man does not make one an understanding and sympathetic manager. It is more likely to be considered by senior Asian managers as a crude token or a futile gesture to camouflage insincerity. One is more likely to earn respect by being open and candid in expressing a lack of personal conviction about such practices. There is so much more to share than beliefs in superstition. From the standpoint of practical management, one certainly cannot ascribe failures to evil omens. When a worker has a fatal accident at a construction site, the introduction of more stringent safety procedures may be the solution rather than the propitiation of disgruntled spirits. Faith in a manager's honest concern about their welfare is more important to the vast majority of employees today than symbolic gestures. This, however, does not apply to genuine religious ceremonies which are an established custom, such as a Buddhist ceremony at the opening of a new office in Thailand, or a Shinto blessing for the start of a new plant in Japan.

7   Be careful of liaisons

Bob Veltman had been in Singapore barely a week. Though his new job as head of the shipping division at the international company was challenging enough, he had nothing to do in his free time. Bored and lonely and unable to face another evening by himself, he invited Maria Rajan, his boss's secretary, to join him for a drink after work. It was a spur-of-the-moment gesture, but they spent a pleasant evening together and agreed to meet again. Bob was a good-looking, carefree bachelor from Amsterdam; Maria, from an Indian Catholic family, was a quarter Welsh on her mother's side and was considered stunningly beautiful. As their relationship developed, and they were often seen in each other's company, people in the office began to notice. Bob's boss, who had been in Asia several years and recognised the danger signals, hoped it was only a passing phase. Meanwhile, Maria took the important step of inviting Bob home to meet her parents. He liked them and was flattered by the way they treated him as an honoured guest. Bob did not realise how the friendship was being misinterpreted. Maria's father, a prosperous foreign exchange dealer, was an educated man—indeed, his own father had struggled hard to put him through college—but a higher standard of living had not changed traditional family values. When Maria brought Bob home, her parents naturally assumed they were planning to get engaged. But Bob was young and had given no thought to settling down. As far as he was concerned, Maria was just his girlfriend, someone he liked a lot. The more they were seen together the more the poor girl's position was compromised. Bob's boss soon realised what had happened. Maria's reputation and her family's honour were at stake. He confronted the astonished Bob, who assured him that he and Maria were just good friends. By now, however, everybody in the office was talking about how cruelly the heartless Bob was using innocent Maria. After all, the pair had been observed together at social clubs and parties, on occasion quite late. Without understanding how, Bob found himself at the centre of a scandal. It became impossible for Maria to continue as secretary of the company's chief executive. When she resigned, her colleagues felt sympathy for her and anger at Bob—some refused to speak to him. Finally, his boss called him one day and told him about an opening in the Jakarta office which afforded an opportunity to expand his work experience. This was not really so, because the Singapore position was the more senior. However, Bob soon saw that there was no choice. Head office was informed and the transfer dealt quite a blow to Bob's career.

The incident might have been less tragic had Maria come from a more modern family background, but it would still have been unpleasant for Bob. Nobody back in Amsterdam had explained to him about social constraints in Asia and how they continue to coexist with modern attitudes. Attractive dress, striking make-up, and informal behaviour on the part of female employees can be dangerous for expatriates uninitiated in Asian cultures. Looks and demeanour can easily be misconstrued as an invitation to a familiarity beyond the acceptable norm in their social circles.

8   Remain calm and in control

In Asia, good managers are expected to display inner calm and control over their environment. They should not appear consumed by work. Their ideal is to find harmony, inner and external. In the age of the microchip, the Japanese still go cherry-blossom viewing. Koreans call their country the 'Land of Morning Calm'. Confucianism and Buddhism rank peace and order high among the desired goals. Hinduism teaches detachment. Asian employees feel uncomfortable with blatant ambition and undignified rush; even talking fast is considered glib. Jeremy Pickle was always in a rush. After a meeting with a Chinese official he complained about the delay in making a decision. As the official later remarked to the Asian manager accompanying Pickle, 'If he spoke a little slower, we'd make faster progress.'

Speed is not always considered a sign of efficiency in Asia; often it is associated with rudeness. The speed syndrome fills people with anxiety and tension and they find it unpleasant. In addition, anger, worry, and fear are considered unworthy of a good leader. Asian managers believe that a high standard of living and a top salary make many expatriate managers perpetually apprehensive of being unable to afford their lifestyles if something goes wrong. Such fear results in constant stress and tension, thus seriously affecting their peace of mind. There is so much in Asian philosophy that puts a high premium on taking control of one's self. Zen philosophy, for instance, teaches that when we suffer fear, anxiety, or nervous anticipation, we are living in the past or the future. We must live in the present. In a Zen story, two monks approaching a river see a beautiful woman unable to cross by herself. Without a word, the older monk picks her up and carries her across. 'How could you, a monk, even think of holding a woman in your arms?' asks the younger one angrily. 'I put her down at the roadside,' replies the older monk. 'Are you still carrying her?'

The Gita tells us to do our duty without thinking about results. Mahatma Gandhi translated it in his discourses: 'Without worrying about the fruit of action, a man must devote himself to the performance of his duty with an evenness of temper. This is yoga, or skill in action. The success of an act lies in performing it, and not in the result, whatever it is.'

In Raja Yoga one learns how the weeding out of undesirable characteristics is accompanied by the cultivation of desirable ones. To overcome fear, one must concentrate upon the ideal of courage. One must train until one acquires the power of conscious direction of the sub-conscious mind. 'The mind is plastic to him who knows the secret of its manipulation,' says Yogi Ramacharaka. 'We are the makers, preservers, and destroyers of our personal thought-world.'

There is no dearth of training programs available to managers today to cope with stress. One of them is called the Silva Mind Control Method. In this program participants are taught the discipline of dynamic meditation and the ability to relax within seconds by descending to the 'second level of consciousness, just short of sleep, called the alpha level'. They also learn to focus on the desired result rather than a negative situation, and to tap into the creative part of the brain, a form of 'inner visioning'. Once you have released most of the tension, you tend to make a greater number of correct decisions, says a program instructor. First your mind conceives of something and then you begin to believe you can do it. After that you build up the expectation that it will happen. Then you claim the result by visualising it in a specially trained way. Finally you go out and do it.

9   Be an attentive listener

Try to be a good listener. Your Asian associates will be less direct in conversation than you are used to at head office. Be patient and you will gradually learn to understand the nuances that are intended to be conveyed. The cost of poor listening can be high. Listening is not merely an act of closing the office door and letting someone speak without interruption. Nor is it a question of just looking interested and avoiding negative gestures. Important as they are, these bits of etiquette constitute mere 'passive' listening. The real damage occurs when this becomes a substitute for active attention, which enables co-workers to feel free to throw up new ideas. Good listening is an act of faith that unites supervisors and subordinates, leaders and followers, in a well-knit team.

This can, however, be thwarted by the barrier of rank: people are often reluctant to talk freely to senior managers. Another danger lies in short attention-spans, a curse afflicting most busy managers. They may listen alertly at first, then monopolise the discourse, or disconcertingly jump to a conclusion. 'Are you saying we should abort this plan?' the boss might ask before the issue can be made clear. A frequent obstacle, too, is simple misunderstanding. A Malaysian senior official once told me about the debacle of a meeting he had experienced with the visiting executive of a large corporation, who had sought the session to gain a helpful viewpoint on local equity. But the visitor took up most of the time in explaining how the company's Malaysian operations fitted in with its worldwide structure. Afterwards he griped to his local manager that the host listened poorly. The 'poor listener' thought the same about him!

By far the largest barriers, however, are cultural. To many Westerners, aggressive questioning is a normal technique when challenging an idea or statement. To others, however, it may look confrontational. I recall a meeting years ago at which a Japanese manager forecast that the yen would rise to what then seemed an unbelievable level. A couple of sceptics pounced on him with a barrage of questions. He cited many reasons, but recoiled from what he saw as hostile crossfire. He cut his argument short, he told me later, for fear of appearing 'too nationalistic'. The incident shows how an ignorance of cultural differences can impede the flow of ideas. A Thai or a Malay manager would probably have reacted similarly.

The art of genuine listening can be cultivated in many ways. One is to come up with as many points as possible in favour of what someone is proposing. A manager once told me that he religiously forces himself to cite at least two virtues in an idea no matter how impractical the idea may seem at first. It is easier to deal with the drawbacks of a proposal once its merits have been clearly established. Another vital factor in attentive listening is the creation of interpersonal and cross-cultural rapports. Good managers make a discussion interesting, rather than intimidating, to a subordinate. They prod gently, swap stories, show concern, motivate, and often end up making the exchange a memorable one. As they listen, they build trust, encourage innovation and sort out priorities. They use company folklore to illustrate their vision. They use listening to enhance personal relationships. No problem is too petty for them if it is large for the person it affects. Above all, good managers invariably follow up their words with action. Managers who talk more than they listen should not be surprised if they achieve far fewer positive results.

10   Talk to people face to face

Asian societies are based on personal relationships. Nothing confuses Asian managers more than an impersonal memo. Of all the styles of management, they find this the most invidious. Nothing destroys the boss-subordinate relationship more thoroughly or more wantonly than the imperious managerial missive. When Khun Tawon, head of the accounting division of an international company in Bangkok, saw a memo from his new boss, he could not believe his eyes. 'It has been brought to my notice,' it read, 'that employees in your division habitually put in overtime. This practice is to be stopped forthwith.' This is typical of senior managers unable or unwilling to establish reasonable working relationships with those they work with. It is cold, impersonal, and arrogant—a manager elevating himself to master. Memos like that immediately relegate people to subservient roles and poison the spirit of team-building. Managers who expect subordinates to follow written dictates without deviation are often inadequate both as human beings and as executives. They usually adopt this destructive method of communication because they are driven by organisation charts. To them, the only effective way of communicating is for the boxes at the top of the chart to 'talk' down to the boxes at lower levels—to order, to command, to insist on everyone falling in line.

Successful managerial leaders don't resort to memos. They talk to people—face to face, person to person. They are organisational morale builders: they respect the individual, not only for what he is today, but also for what he can be tomorrow. They are organisational instigators: they spread the idea that people do their best because they want to improve themselves, not because they are afraid of the boss. To them, creativity is the child of a company's vision and of the employees' free response to it. Managerial leaders are powerful catalysts; they seduce people to a new faith.

Herb Moser was one of the most prolific memo writers I have ever known. Before coming to Asia, Moser had spent his entire career at manufacturing plants and had done well in his last job as a factory manager. He used to write a lot of memos, to be sure, but he was dealing with shift superintendents, storemen, and machine watchers. When he arrived at the Asian head office of Westbig Corporation, he found himself dealing with people representing a whole continent in transition. These were not the kind of people who could be led by memo. But that was the only method he knew. 'I have been advised that you have been using your secretary for personal work,' wrote Moser to an Asian department manager. From that day, the man's relationship with Moser changed irrevocably. Why did Moser not write to other department heads? he wondered. Would he have sent that memo if I had been an expatriate? Why didn't he talk to me first? The secretary had not complained. A newcomer in the employee relations department had been asked to find out whether the number of secretaries could be reduced and Moser had decided to write a couple of memos to 'solve the situation'. But 'solving' a problem by writing a memo is an act of corporate cowardice. It doesn't invite the recipient to explain their position. It says, 'I don't want a dialogue. I want you to do as you are told.' It uses fear rather than fairness; it emphasises position over person. The irony is that it is people like Moser who are also the ones fond of sending out memos that say 'People are our greatest asset.' Khun Tawon is generally a mild person, but he was outraged when he told me about the memo concerning overtime. He was convinced that overtime was necessary because of understaffing in his division. 'I don't think the idiot was interested in understanding my problem. He didn't even give me the chance to explain.' Tawon echoed the other Asian manager's cry, 'Why didn't he talk to me?' The truth of the matter is that memo writers are not really interested in solving problems—they are consumed by the need to assert their position. They probably have never been told that management by memos is the worst possible way to manage.

14 Managing day-to-day relationships

Expatriates often think Asians are ultra-sensitive about how others behave towards them. They feel exasperated by the cumbersome protocol demanded in everyday conduct and behaviour. However, to succeed as a multinational manager in Asia, one cannot afford to remain unaware of the sensitive spots. Offence can easily be caused by ignoring what is regarded as ordinary politeness and courtesy. Even a simple action may sometimes appear condescending and patronising. A reputation of being snooty may be earned by responding to a greeting with a faraway look. To a slighted subordinate that may signify a preoccupation with weightier matters. Grievous pain could be caused by a casual remark uttered with a hint of sarcasm about the colour of one's tie. An over-protective secretary could create enormous ill-feeling by acting as a barrier. Here are 25 tips for survival and success in day-to-day business relationships.

1 Avoid put-downs

Be careful that what you say and do is not taken as a put-down. Your smile at a mispronounced English word can be easily mistaken for a sneer. For instance, a Chinese female middle manager could not pronounce 'February' correctly—this always amused her expatriate boss, much to the great embarrassment of everybody else. Another Asian manager made a remark about taxes at a meeting which was at variance with the views of an American manager. Cupping his ear, the American asked, 'What did you say, Texas?' The Asian manager was deeply hurt. Don't try to make a person repeat a word with which he or she is having a problem. A young manager was once making a presentation on the environmental impact of a new plant. Most people present thought it was tactless of the chairperson to make him pronounce the word 'hazardous' twice, even though everybody could understand it anyway.

One of Jeremy Pickle's favourite put-downs which annoyed everyone was to tell a person in the middle of a report that he was not interested in minutiae. His sarcastic remarks and careless attempts at witticism were also greatly disliked. When the Asian manager of an affiliate called for approval to close the office earlier in honour of a national leader who had passed away, Pickle remarked, 'I am not a specialist in mourning.' The manager told everyone about it and the whole office was appalled.

On another occasion, at the opening of a new office, Pickle congratulated everyone for doing a good job. He singled out the head of the mail-room and asked him to come over to the microphone. The poor fellow suffered from a slight deformity in one leg and as he limped his way up, Pickle announced to the gathering, 'He dropped a filing cabinet on his foot.' Nobody laughed. When the woman editor of a company magazine once asked him for suggestions, he proposed publishing recipes for different types of food in the region. She felt outraged at the male chauvinistic remark.

Using one's secretary to make telephone calls can be mistaken as an overbearing act. A secretary rings a person with whom her employer does frequent business and asks him to wait. After a long pause she announces that Mr Gerald Plum is now in a meeting and that she will call back later. This annoys Cecelia Lo whose firm is a relative newcomer to a competitive industry. Plum, by contrast, is a division head with an old trading and distribution company. The telephone system in Lo's outfit puts through calls directly without mediation by an operator, let alone a secretary. Managers in a large company may not take it amiss if the chief executive's secretary phones to relay the boss's wish to see them. In a small company, the action could be considered pompous.

Remarks with racial overtones can be dangerous even if they are made without any apparent prejudice. An Australian manager upset several potential clients at his company's cocktail reception in Hong Kong by his remark, 'The Chinese are used to confined spaces. We have seven people in a room 20 foot by 6 foot in our new office.'

2   Don't expect people to take sides

Asians feel uneasy about taking sides in a heated argument. A typical example is the continuing debate about trade friction between the USA and Japan. Barry Chu, a senior local manager with an international company, recently invited me to dinner to meet some visitors from his New York head office. These executives had stopped over in Tokyo for a few days. Overwhelmed, they talked of little else. 'I was surprised at the arrogance of the people we met,' said John Norton, a vice president. 'The strong yen has gone to their heads. They would have you believe Japan is blameless.' I could see Chu becoming increasingly uncomfortable as the talk turned to Japan's 'free ride' in defence, the scale of Japanese investment in the USA, and the inevitability of protectionism. Such a conversation puts many Asian managers in an emotional dilemma. As they see it, both countries are enormously successful and neither should suffer by comparison. They are both unique in their own ways and many of the attributes of both are admired by Asians. The USA revels in the celebration of the individual. Japan exults in its social cohesion. Americans are open, frank, and straightforward. Japanese are polite, indirect, and circumspect. The corporate mission in the USA is to make money for the shareholders. In Japan it is to ensure the longevity of the company and to protect employment. Americans do not view business in patriotic terms, but Japanese treat industrial performance on a par with national security. American consumers aggressively buy the best and the cheapest. Japanese docilely fork out the highest prices in the world. The USA is multi-ethnic, Japan is homogeneous.

To people like Chu, the answer to the deficit problem does not lie in changing each other's societies. The worst thing an expatriate manager can do in the face of such sentiments is to accuse an Asian manager of being anti-American or anti-Western. Simply because people don't agree with you on an issue does not mean they reject the values of the society to which you belong.

3 Keep communication channels open

Remember that rumours will take over if you don't establish some system of open communication in the office. Instead of facing this fact, some managers waste a lot of time in trying to identify sources and putting rumours down. 'I don't think you will believe me,' said a friend of mine over the phone the other day. 'I have just found out that our general manager's secretary is a spy. She is spying on all of us here. And you know what? She was asked by the old man to do it.' I was quite surprised at the disclosure and tried to make him see a positive side. 'Maybe your general manager is really concerned about employee morale. Isn't it better if he hears things informally before they get out of hand?' He gave a disbelieving grunt, but I pressed on. I reminded him about an earlier crisis. 'You said several people were planning to quit because of the new distribution manager, and then suddenly his behaviour changed. Perhaps,' I went on, 'the old man heard about this fellow through his secretary and gave him a bit of advice.'

But I had to agree that gathering information through the help of an office spy is not the most desirable activity. It creates distrust and destroys any hope of building a team. Gradually people come to know about the spy and begin to feed them unfounded information. When the manager acts on it, he becomes the butt of collective ridicule. You can't kill gossip, and there is no merit in that anyway. Mostly it's innocent—a kind of pastime indulged in by office colleagues. A good manager, however, can certainly create an environment in which people are kept informed and feel able to express their concerns.

4 Differentiate between 'yes' and 'no'

Some time ago a couple of American friends who had lived in China gave me a manuscript to read before sending it off to a prospective publisher. Provisionally titled *A Key to what they really mean in China*, the work explains how certain terms and phrases can denote a wide range of meanings. Offering humorous glimpses behind the great wall of language, they stress that learning what is *meant* rather than what is said is the key to real understanding in China. The first utterance a visitor is most likely to learn is *meiyou*. Its literal meaning is 'not have', but it can mean many different things: 'We have some, but we are saving them for special customers'; 'We cannot be bothered to find them because we have no incentive to do so'; 'If you are persistent and prepared to wait, we may be able to locate some'; 'You should have come earlier'; 'It's only for display'; 'The manager hasn't given us the latest price list'; 'We have, but the man with the key is not here.'

Similarly *deng yi xia* ('wait a moment') could mean any of the following: 'I don't know how long this is going to take'; 'I need to get the answer from my colleague'; 'We have to hold a private meeting to discuss it'. The phrase *mei you wen ti* ('no problem') could mean; 'Your problems have just begun but I don't know how to tell you'; 'Don't worry, you will *eventually* get there'; 'If we all believe it will work out, then maybe it will.' For the real nuance, insist the authors, you must pay attention to what the speaker is trying to tell you and not what you *want* to hear. A cartoon on the cover reinforces this point. An anxious-looking pair of Western businessmen are sitting opposite their poker-faced Chinese counterparts over a negotiating table. The foreign boss whispers to his junior, 'Is it possible to ask if their "maybe" really means "maybe", or does it mean "no" or "probably no" or "possibly" or "definitely not"?'

5   Don't be alarmed by different odds

While gambling is not usually part of the social fabric in Asia, there is in general considerable tolerance for betting. In the excitement of high stakes, discretion is sometimes thrown to the wind. This tends to alarm foreign managers. They expect middle managers to exhibit sober judgment and to support their decisions with sound facts and solid figures. So when they see these same employees displaying the opposite qualities during leisure hours, they are apt to draw wrong conclusions.

Bill Long, a department head at an international company, was invited to go to the races with two of his product managers. He studied the form briefly and decided to back a couple of favourites. But Andrew Lam and Sato-san, he was surprised to see, kept going for long odds with substantial bets. Bill was concerned at the money the two were losing. Happily, the evening ended well when Andrew's final pick came in at a hundred to one and they went to dinner to celebrate. 'Do you always bet like that?' Bill asked. 'Well,' replied Andrew, still flushed with success 'what's the point of putting down a hundred dollars to win a hundred? Where's the excitement in that?' Bill, a relative newcomer to Asia, couldn't really be blamed for thinking his associates were compulsive gamblers. At work he began to doubt their judgment. When Sato presented preliminary figures on a new investment project, Bill was astounded by the discounted cash flow number. 'Are you sure you can justify the DCF to the management committee?' he asked disbelievingly. Sato looked at his calculations with a characteristically bruised look. 'Well, to be precise it comes to 39.89, but I've rounded it up to 40.' Bill simply couldn't reconcile Sato's apparently carefree flinging around of money at the track with his uncompromising numerical precision at work. How could a man live with such a finely controlled dichotomy? In time he was to discover that Andrew Lam was amazingly conservative at credit control and balanced his inventories with projected demand so well that one could only marvel at his level-headed competence. Obviously, gambling was *not* a way of life with these men. It's true that when they gamble, they put aside the discipline of company controller or treasurer, but they are adept at using a quite different standard at work.

6   Don't name-drop to intimidate

When expatriates want business from Asian managers, they must be careful how they try to influence their decisions. An expatriate insurance executive calls on Abdul Ishaq, a manager with an international company in Kuala Lumpur. As he presents his calling card, he mentions that he enjoyed the game of golf he had with Ishaq's European boss the previous weekend. An American publisher of an Asian business magazine happens to sit next to Kwok Siu Lun at a Chamber of Commerce luncheon in Hong Kong and spends most of the time talking about people he knows in the New York head office of Kwok's company. Next day, with his local advertising manager in tow, he calls on Kwok and wants to know why he has stopped advertising.

On the surface, it may appear that there's nothing wrong with name-dropping. After all, peddling influence is a time-honoured method of trying to win a business deal, but it's a great mistake to do it in a manner that is intimidating. And it can be particularly insulting when the name-dropping *precedes* a presentation of the merits of a product or service. Asian managers increasingly take pride in being professional. Not long ago, I had a talk with Jane Flowers, a successful British advertising executive whose approach with Asian managers proves that, contrary to general belief, pulling strings is not necessary. She said that most of the Asian managers she meets have made it to the top in the face of severe competition. They are dedicated to their work and don't make business decisions lightly.

7   Be sensitive to Atlantic cross-fire

Renato is an employee relations assistant at the regional office of a large American company. He was educated in the USA and feels more comfortable with Americans than with Europeans. At his office there are British and French senior executives, but their relationship with Americans is always tense. The Frenchman is forever deriding the 'lack of culture' among Americans, and the English manager constantly says Americans are naive and inexperienced in dealing with Asians. Underlying this friction, Renato senses the frustration of Europeans working for a firm whose top management is American. When talking to Renato, each side runs the other down and he is caught in the cross-fire. Of course, Renato realises he is working for an American company, even though it calls itself multinational. Head office management will always be American. His European colleagues are obviously frustrated because they enjoy only a semblance of power. Nevertheless, he is also aware that a European colleague may one day have a posting at the head office which could lead to a sudden and dramatic change in attitude. The French manager who used to bemoan the lack of culture of Americans was in fact assigned to New York. Not long afterwards he appeared in the company in-house magazine saying how impressed he was with the high degree of culture in the USA. Asian managers don't want to be caught in the Atlantic cross-fire. They know it is not in their interest to take sides. They have seen others fall into the trap and hurt their careers.

8   Don't fall for the sexist stigma

My friend Jambon had barely said hello over the telephone the other day, when he shot at me this question: 'Do you think I am a sexist?' I knew immediately that something was wrong. He and I go back a few years and it was obvious he didn't want a simple 'yes' or 'no'. So I tried to calm him down by taking an indirect approach. 'Well,' I said hesitatingly, 'all men are sexists up to a point. Depends how you define it.' This didn't help at all. 'Okay, you define it for me,' he demanded. So I proceeded to describe a few situations that might characterise a man as sexist: one who habitually addresses his remarks only to male companions, ignoring the presence of a female in the group; a manager who asks the only female at a meeting to check if coffee is ready; a boss who calls his secretary 'cutie'. But Jambon was still unsatisfied. Pressed to go on, I fell back on a very basic definition. 'A sexist is a man who does not respect women and treats them as objects,' I pronounced. 'Of course, in the office, sexism can also constitute discrimination.' This seemed to be what Jambon was after. 'That's exactly what has happened,' he said. 'Dorothy has just accused me of it.' Jambon had given me some news about her a week earlier. The company's head office had assigned her to help train a couple of new women assistants in his department. She had just taken them out to lunch and returned around 3.30 pm with a bill for, among other things, two bottles of fairly expensive wine. 'I told her I'd not approve the bill', Jambon explained hotly. An argument had ensued, it seems, and she had stalked out insisting that the expense would never have been questioned had it been incurred by a man.

Fortunately, the matter was resolved later in the afternoon, when the wine's effect had worn off and Dorothy was less confrontational. But the incident illustrates that because of the male chauvinist image of Asian men, it is easy for a visitor, especially a woman, to jump to conclusions. Most Asians go out of their way to be polite to Western women. They show them courtesies they would probably feel awkward about extending to women of their own culture. In the latter case, it simply isn't the custom. But that doesn't make Asian men inconsiderate. No one claims there is the same degree of equality between the sexes in Asia as in Europe or the USA—but that does not mean all Asian men are slave-drivers holding their women in bondage. Unfortunately, it is easy for casual observers to form such an impression, particularly from the viewpoint of contemporary Western experience.

9   Keep your fitness fad private

Expatriate middle managers who rush madly to fit in a strenuous game of squash between a sandwich and a monthly budget meeting are simply trying to appear to be in fashion. In the view of Asian managers, they are caught up in an obsession with physical fitness that is as fanatical as the rat race for success. They consider a sport more a status symbol than a means for social and physical relaxation. Expatriate middle managers use it as a badge of success. In the mornings they can be seen in the office lifts carrying their sports bags with rackets bulging conspicuously out. At lunchtime, while lesser mortals slouch to the nearest fast-food outlet, this elite brigade scatters for quick rounds of squash. In the evening they can't get away fast enough for a jog or a few brisk lengths in their condominium pools. Some become a bore by talking of nothing else than their favourite sport. Others think it chic to dwell on health food, dieting, the dangers of high cholesterol, and similar real or imagined health hazards. Nobody questions that long working hours, travel, and the competitive grind of business today demand more attention to health. But health consciousness should not go overboard. Instead of running around with sports bag during the lunch break, it would be far better to establish a daily regimen of morning exercise before work. Remember, it's your health that ultimately counts, not the public display of it.

10   Cooperate before competing

A few years ago I had fixed a game of golf with the manager of the Asian subsidiary of an international company. He asked if he could bring his teenage son along. I was delighted and looked forward to a pleasant outing. The manager was a good golfer, but his 15–year old son had a hard struggle to keep up. It was a hot day and he began to fade in the middle of the back nine. His father kept on pushing him, angrily telling him to concentrate and try harder. By the end of the game the youngster was just about broken and near to tears. The atmosphere of work-competitiveness had been extended to a domestic and social situation. Many managers are obsessed with using competition to motivate subordinates, judge their behaviour, and evaluate their performances. They forget that in most human endeavours you must learn to cooperate before you can compete. They may watch inspirational videos that compare companies to symphony orchestras, but when they go back to their offices, they fight like street-cats. One fine-tuned foreign company I know of has been practically destroyed by its managers' in-fighting. After the company's reorganisation there was no clear leader. Three or four top managers of the same level fought it out while the employees watched helplessly. Those managers were doing what they had been trained to do.

Yet it is cooperation, not competition, that breeds real team leaders. Striving towards a shared goal brings out the best in people. When the stress is solely on individual achievement, this power is lost. From an Asian perspective, the practice of equating success with victory is unsatisfying. Superior performance does not always require competition. When employees are not divided into winners and losers, higher morale and productivity often result. In a competitive atmosphere, by contrast, your colleagues hope to see you fail. In the quest for quality and the pursuit of perfection, the challenge should be to improve ourselves, not to beat someone else. As Ito Momoko, a senior executive of Energy Conservation Devices, puts it, 'If you compete against yourself, the challenge never ends'.

11   Don't take courtesy for granted

As the president and his wife step from the plane, the band srikes up a greeting. Decked with garlands, the honoured guests pass along the welcoming line, pausing here and there to shake hands, and enter the VIP lounge. The limousine draws up and the presidential convoy speeds into town. No, this not a state visit—simply a stop on the Asian itinerary of the CEO of a big multinational. In Singapore, oversized bouquets are waiting in the garden suite of the Shangri-La. In Bangkok, company cars escort them to the Oriental, where their suite is pre-stocked with their favourite drinks. In New Delhi, a customer arranges a champagne reception at the Taj. In Karachi, where drinking is forbidden, the cocktail party at the local manager's home is attended by senior government officials. Everywhere, special arrangements speed clearance through immigration and customs. Local managers personally double-check every moment of the tour.

What are the visitors to make of all this? Ordinary Eastern courtesy—or deference towards distinguished Westerners? Traditional Asian hospitality—or obsequiousness to the big boss? Clearly Asian standards of courtesy differ from Western ones. Politeness in business, to be sure, derives largely from general society, so it is easier to extend special attention to guests when airport and hotel personnel are used to it. But it is so easy to misunderstand this hospitality.

In part, business courtesy is ordinary politeness, and in part, maintaining cordial relationships—through exchanging gifts and conveying regards of acquaintances. There is another kind of courtesy—that offered by managers in an attempt to ingratiate themselves with their superiors. Courtesy out of deference to Westerners is less likely today. But what most sets Asian courtesy apart is its deep-rooted traditional hospitality towards guests. This demands that one look after guests even at the cost of personal discomfort. If you protest, your host will reply simply that you are his guest. Most Asian managers would like their hospitality to be seen in this light and may be uncomfortable if the visitor doesn't understand. It is important to recognise this cultural aspect and respond appropriately, by being even lavish in praise. It transcends your relationship as a boss and in Asia it is a sign of ill-breeding to take courtesy for granted because of your position. The Western business world operates differently. The host may not be at the airport when the Asian manager visits Europe or the USA. The hotel may fall short of expectations and there may be no special program for the evening. Experienced Asian managers don't expect reciprocity, only appreciation of a deep cultural trait.

12   Be careful about community service

Many managers make a valuable contribution of one kind or another to society. They give freely of their time and expertise to help charities, clubs or professional bodies. They work selflessly in support of the arts, education, sport, or culture. Often the task is thankless, with little reward or recognition. Even their motives are sometimes misunderstood and instead of earning gratitude, these managers can end up making themselves unpopular. I recall, for example, the case of a career-conscious bank executive who was on the management committee of a chamber of commerce which gave him the job of reviving a dormant community relations program. He convened a meeting, to which many companies sent representatives, but he had to hurry away early to an appointment. Apologising cursorily, he asked the group to carry on without him. This certainly did not endear him or his bank to the people who had taken the trouble to attend.

Another instance concerns a friend of mine, an enlightened senior manager, who was invited to join the advisory board of a local university. He was eminently suited to the position and was keen to help the cause. But he was soon disillusioned. Another member, head of an old trading house, had reactionary views. 'We in industry must decide how many locals with higher education we need,' this man pronounced during a discussion about a proposed new wing. My friend was appalled. As a young man he had held two part-time jobs to pay for his education. He had accepted the university's invitation in the hope that he would be able to help deserving youth—not to be party to some grand social manipulation. Yet another manager found that representation on a well-known charity's committee was chiefly thought of as a way of becoming part of the social elite. People vied for membership to gain publicity. Disbursement of funds was mechanical and bureaucratic and most committee members had little knowledge of, or sympathy with, the needy.

There is a lesson to be learnt here for the well-meaning manager. First, make sure you have the time and patience for public service. Working with elected bodies requires a temperament quite different from that needed when working in an office. You must deal with people who differ widely in educational background, occupation, mission, and motive. Second, be clear about what you want to contribute. It is best to limit your role at first to professional help. You can enhance this role if you find yourself among like-minded people or disengage if there is too much discord. Third, do not be too closely identified for too long with any one organisation. Fourth, avoid becoming prominent in a social organisation which tends to be sectarian. The president of a club not open to all nationalities can be embarrassed if a colleague's application to join is turned down.

In the right circumstances, voluntary work can be both personally satisfying and a credit to one's company. There are so many spheres of life in Asia in which professional managers can help. Asians unfortunately lack the strong tradition of social service such as is found in the USA. Education—especially business schools—is clearly a field worthy of support. Giving lectures, providing scholarships, helping to raise funds, and supporting research are more worthwhile than striving to be in the social limelight.

13   Don't over-emphasise your contacts

Despite the importance of personal relationships, don't let your Asian colleagues convince you that contacts are everything. Sometimes they exploit this impression to gain special privileges. A Filipino manager of a foreign company's local subsidiary sent the following justification for a golf club corporate debenture to his regional office: 'Wack Wack is the club that offers the best contacts in the Philippines for informal interaction with the leaders of government. The contacts I personally made at this club in the past account for a number of important accommodations by government, eg. positive responses to our applications for foreign exchange covering raw materials importations under tightly controlled Forex conditions.' He also recommended that the company executive vice president on his forthcoming visit to Manila should bring a set of graphite shaft clubs for President Marcos. 'He should have been a caddy master,' a senior Asian manager observes wryly, 'rather than the Philippines manager of one of the world's largest companies.'

A Japanese manager with a foreign company once told visitors from head office that his department had established a system through which it could obtain the Liberal Democratic Party's position papers on important issues in advance. He pointed out that these papers represented the thinking stage rather than the policy-making stage. His department took special care to destroy the covers of these reports and did not reveal the source to management. He stressed that access to these papers was the result of 'years of contacts, efforts and energy'. The danger of such practices is that Asian managers begin to see their worth to the company in terms of influence-peddling rather than professional competence.

The same concept of a cosy relationship can often colour judgment in important matters. One company appointed an outside director in a Southeast country because he was the father-in-law of the prime minister. Another company reported on the political outlook after the death of the incumbent prime minister: 'It is too early to say what this change in leadership might bring but the fact that the new prime minister is the brother-in-law of the previous one tends to suggest a continuation of past policies, at least in the short term.' Many leaders brought down by close relatives would envy such a simplistic assessment of Asian politics.

An expatriate manager must also be careful not to judge openly the leading politicians on the basis of their positive or negative stance towards the company's business alone. One manager wrote down on a newspaper clipping which carried an item about the death of a South Asian minister, 'This was the bad guy in the pricing negotiation flap,' and sent it to the regional president who marked 'good riddance' on it and circulated it to several managers. The Asians among them were disgusted.

14 Be discreet about offering domestic advice

Even when you know an Asian manager well, be careful in offering advice on domestic and family matters. The right and wrong solutions are based not on common sense or logic but tradition, face, and family pride. An expatriate once urged an Asian manager to ask his son studying in the USA to get some part-time work to help defray the high cost. To him it appeared to be a sensible suggestion. But as the Asian manager knew his son, being a foreigner, could only get 'menial' jobs like waiting in the college cafeteria or helping with the collection of dustbins, he was quite upset. The family had not sent the eldest son to the USA for college education to work as a labourer.

On another occasion an Australian advised a Japanese manager and his wife on how to handle their teenage son who was slipping in his studies. His own son had become a 'layabout', the Australian told them, and he was not going to do anything about it. He had withdrawn all financial support. He wanted his son to learn from experience even if it meant taking the risk that it would ruin his life. Given the strong family structure in Japan, in particular mothers' fierce devotion to their children, the Japanese couple were astounded. In fact, from that point on they could never really consider the Australian as a particularly good person.

15   Avoid expletives

There was a time when an expletive was pardonable only in extenuating circumstances—a finger caught in the car door or coffee spilled on a Kashan carpet. Today people swear at everything. Even the office is a free-fire zone. Managers feel macho when they use salty language. Winning a contract is as good a reason as losing one. No longer limited to fishwives and foot soldiers, the blue oath has become common currency among many modern managers.

The golden rule in the office is that you must never use foul language in anger or with colleagues you don't know well. Even otherwise, it's generally frowned upon. There are exceptions however—you may use it occasionally to embellish a story, create effect, attract attention, or to express utter frustration. It's invariably condoned as a deflator of pompous types, as evidenced by the existence of some very colourful Asian terms for such a person. It can be put to effective use by a supervisor to achieve a friendly emphasis. Nothing is more reassuring to an anxious subordinate than to be told by his boss not to (expletive deleted) worry about it. But one must be quite discriminating about profanity. People who indulge in it as a matter of course often become a crushing bore to their colleagues.

16   Don't mix only with Westernised Asians

It is very easy for expatriate managers to feel closer to those Asians who are more Westernised. Be careful that you don't do it in too obvious a manner, especially in choosing the people you socialise with. You are unlikely to enrich your knowledge or experience of local culture by being surrounded with such people. If, as a senior executive, you are called upon to choose an Asian manager as a spokesperson of the company, choose a lesser Westernised person. Subconsciously, the Asian media reporters react negatively to managers who appear to be carbon-copies of American or European executives. These managers are also liable to make statements, which though factual, come over as boasting. Lesser Westernised managers are more modest.

17   Control your anger

You have to lose your temper with an Asian associate only once and he or she will never forgive you. I once knew a manager who was by nature confrontational. Asians dreaded him because every discussion with him turned into an argument which he always won because others backed off when he lost his temper. You must be especially careful with people who are lower down in the hierarchy. I asked Khun Banchong, manager of Thai Chemicals Corporation, if he got quite angry when somebody made a mistake. 'Well, at first you feel anger,' he said. 'But it all depends on the type of mistake. It is also important at which level the mistake takes place. At the unskilled or lower level, you may have done much good in the past, but if you show your anger even once, all the past kindness is washed out.'

18   Don't take offence at 'fat' remarks

Asians feel that foreigners, especially women, are too sensitive about their weight. Asians don't look upon fatness as something of which one should be ashamed. A Pakistani manager's wife once told the wife of an expatriate manager at a party that she had become fat since the last time she saw her. In Western society such a remark would be considered quite rude, but she did not mean it as an insult. A manager once asked his Malay gardener to describe the person who had delivered a message. 'Was he a fat fellow?' he enquired. 'Yes, a little fat, like Mrs Robins,' the gardener replied, pointing to the manager's wife sitting on the porch.

19   Don't 'prioritise'

Try to avoid terms like 'prioritise' or 'strategise'; their use indicates a lack of maturity and dehumanises your relations with associates. The worst possible term is 'at this point in time'. It's such a pretentious phrase. It tries to give a milestone quality to a non-event. It's not going to win you friends in Asia at any time.

20   Communicate through gifts

Gift-giving is an important means of communication in most traditional societies of Asia, particularly in Japan. Gifts are exchanged to smooth human relations. Parents, company superiors, business clients, and teachers are the most likely recipients. Every Asian country has festivals during which it is customary to offer gifts. Often the practice is rooted in ancient religious rituals—offerings of food to the gods which were shared among the worshippers. The Japanese attach great importance to the traditional semi-annual exchange of gifts: *chugen* in the summertime and *seibo* at the end of the year.

21   Don't anglicise names

You should be sensitive to the correct pronounciation of a person's name. Also learn to distinguish between their first and the last name. Normally a Japanese or a Chinese will show their surname first on the calling card. But many follow the Western practice and put their surname last. Avoid anglicising a person's name. Many people in Hong Kong, for instance, have an English first name. But they are now using their Chinese names more frequently, often in combination with the English name, such as Peter Chu Man-Shing. Man-Shing is the first name.

22   Avoid 'boring' subjects

Some subjects may appear to be quite sensational, especially when you are new to Asia, but don't forget they may be quite boring to your Asian friends and colleagues. Avoid subjects such as the fingerprinting of foreigners in Japan, bride-burning in India, and corruption in the Philippines.

23   Don't be impatient with ambiguity

Ambiguity is woven into the fabric of social and political intercourse in many Asian societies. Often the very precise, clear-cut, definitive, and direct response characteristic in the West, particularly in the

USA, is avoided in preference to an indirect approach. This is an art that you can learn and even enjoy after a while.

24   Select your speakers carefully

Be careful about who you invite to company conferences. At one regional meeting a foreign speaker caused great embarrassment by telling jokes about different nationalities. At another meeting the speaker showed an Iacocca video followed by a diatribe against the Japanese, much to the consternation of several managers from the company's Tokyo office. Inspirational speakers may be the fad in the USA, but they are not very popular in Asia and are sometimes seen as an attempt on the part of management to cover up real problems.

25   Don't expect perfection

Perfectionists are not popular with Asians. Extreme perfectionists enjoy making people feel inadequate, filling them with fear instead of inspiration. In their shadow, others wither and die. They jeer at the idea that humility is the safest path to perfection. They can't understand why a great artist might leave a tiny smudge on his painting or a slight dent on a piece of pottery as proof that only God is perfect. They feel superior to everybody else, always blaming others for their own shortcomings. One such manager had a card on his desk that read: 'It's hard to soar with eagles when you are surrounded by turkeys!' In the mind of such a person, minor lapses of efficiency are exaggerated as a sign of cultural deficiency. One must learn to be philosophical. Here's a story to help you remember that things may not be so bad after all. A person once sent some flowers to a friend who had just opened a new business. The flowers arrived and there on the top was a wreath which said, 'Rest in peace.' When this person found out about it, he called the florist and shouted, 'How dare you send such an arrangement! Do you have any idea how embarrassing this is to me?' The florist waited patiently for the man to calm down a bit and then said: 'You think you feel bad? Somewhere in this city today a man was buried with flowers that read "Good luck in your new location!"'

15 Managing the 'pacific century'

Bill Button had read my latest article on multicultural management. 'You are tilting at windmills,' he said. 'Look around this club. Do you see much socialising going on between expats and locals?' Since everyone around the bar was an expatriate, Bill didn't have to wait for my answer. 'If people can't play together, how do you expect them to work together?' he asked. I agreed that mixing with each other during leisure time might be the true measure of cultural integration. But surely, it was unfair to use that particular club—a relic of a bygone age—as a management blueprint for the pacific century. Of course, nobody expected people from dyed-in-the-wool conservative companies to change, even though their managements daily pronounced the need to become international. This did not mean, however, that others were not interested in learning about the barriers and bridges on the road to effective management in a multicultural environment in Asia.

Not long after my encounter with Bill, I met Miles Simple, an old-time resident of Hong Kong. He reacted with incredulity at what he thought was an underlying negative sentiment against expatriates in some of my columns. I explained that every story I had ever used was true—either I myself was a witness or it was told to me by a manager from personal experience. The purpose of including these stories was exactly the reverse of what Simple had thought. It was to encourage a more positive relationship between Asians and expatriates based on an awareness of how Asians felt about certain behaviour patterns of expatriate managers. Management, after all, is the art of getting things done through people. By understanding their sensitivities, an international manager can accomplish much better results. Almost every Asian manager I have interviewed has stressed some aspect of culture or values which, if ignored, can create permanent ill-will. The tragedy is that foreign managers are sometimes not even aware of these situations. A French personnel manager I used to know a few years ago always maintained that people everywhere are motivated primarily by money. I suspect he had developed this belief because he had worked for a multinational throughout his career in North Africa and Asia as an expatriate. He had never worked in his own country as a local employee. If he had, he would have certainly rated a few things higher than money. The gravest mistake a person can make in Asia is to think that poverty and pride cannot co-exist. Ordinary people are quite often motivated by totally non-mercenary considerations. In his book *Managerial Challenge in the Third World*, Syed Mumtaz Saeed says, 'The Third World managerial community will do well by taking stock of its expertise in non-monetary motivation and beginning to use it; it will, thus, rise from the drudgery of managing of mercenaries to the delight of managing men and women with dignity.'

Gaining acceptability

I had an interesting conversation on the subject of financial reward with Ishizuka Masahiko, editor of the *Japan Economic Journal*. He told me how the chairman of the Japanese Chamber of Commerce (head of a large conglomerate) had stressed in a speech that the salary of a chief executive was only eight times the starting pay of a junior employee (in the USA the average top salary is more than 100 times the entry level pay). Western executives, Ishizuka felt, must wonder what motivates Japanese managers to work so hard to get to the top. Motivation in Japan, he said, comes from various other sources: power, status, the joy of running things, or a sense of mission. The compensation for high-ranking government officials, for example, is lower than that of their counterparts in private corporations. Yet the brightest students from Tokyo University want to join government and work up the ladder.

'Why are corporate executives in Western countries so aggressive about financial rewards?' Ishizuka asked. 'If you earn millions of dollars a year, how do you spend it?' Perhaps, the reason was lack of any other mission. There is no other measure by which senior executives can convince themselves they are successful. 'The Japanese don't understand why the Chairman of General Motors has to get so much money. What's he going to do with it? Maybe he is founding a scholarship?' Ishizuka mused. The size of the chairman's salary was disproportionately large for the contribution he made. In the Japanese context, only a small difference was good enough to motivate. 'We don't need such a big difference,' he said. 'In that sense we are a very egalitarian society.' Japanese managers are sensitive to other, more subtle differences.

I was left with the impression that a Japanese chief executive demanding an astronomical compensation will be neither popular nor acceptable. Acceptability by the people one works with is based on many cultural factors and is considered critical in most Asian societies. Paron Israsena, President of Siam Cement Co., said to me, 'When you go up the organisation in Siam Cement, the key word is acceptability.' Of course, the company's personnel-appraisal system measures job performance and potential, but acceptability lends an added critical dimension. 'The reason I rose to the top is that I had acceptability with the board, my peer group and subordinates. It's very clear here,' Paron told me. He earned acceptability through a systematic approach to people development. When he was asked to take over as personnel manager more than ten years ago, things were in pretty poor shape. 'The personnel-management system here was unbearable. In the past they did not manage. They dictated.' Paron was convinced that, given the choice, he would never have chosen the position. 'It was lousy,' he recalls. 'Nobody came and thanked you. Everybody shouted at you and complained and made a big headache.' But after two years he felt that personnel management was the most important function: 'If you look after your people well and train them well, they will bring you all kinds of new techniques, new ideas, and productivity improvement.'

Becoming a mentor

More than formal training, it is the quality of informal coaching that really counts. A friend once singled out an old column of mine in which I had warned about the tendency of some managers to become masters rather than mentors. 'You can't imagine the difference it has made to my life at the office,' Norman confided. 'I was even told by a fellow the other day how much he likes working with me!' Having always thought that Norman fancied himself a master, I wondered what had happened. He explained that he had gone off to explore in detail the meaning of the word 'mentor', and had discovered that it is a senior who acts as coach, counsellor, and sponsor in a younger person's career development. They not only teach job skills but acquaint the protégé with the organisation's lines of power and politics, endowing hierarchical diagrams with a human dimension. They reveal the parallel, 'shadow' kingdom that exists in most companies and show how keys to it may be used. As counsellors, they act as buffers against psychological pressures and help restore confidence. As sponsors, they help position the protégé for advancement.

Though good at their work, Norman's subordinates had no way of knowing the rules by which the corporate game is played. They were unaware of the quirks of senior managers and did not have a feel for the 'political' environment. Norman now spends more time telling his people about the company's plans and thinking. He also enlightens them about possible consequences of company policies to their own futures. Their sense of security in knowing where they stand has now shot up dramatically. Their confidence has been boosted by Norman's frequent feedback of senior management appraisals of their performance. Assistants feel freer to ask the sort of questions that were often swallowed in the past for fear of looking ignorant. Now fewer mistakes are made, and the new team spirit has in turn enabled Norman to talk more frankly. 'A couple of times my secretary had complained about the aggressive attitude of one of my assistants towards her,' he said. 'It bothered me, but I'd let it pass. I didn't want him to become defensive.' Today such defensiveness has fled, and the assistant was actually grateful to be made aware that he couldn't expect to get far by being tactless with secretaries and clerks. Self-reliance is also up sharply. 'Before they used to come to me for decisions,' said Norman. 'Now they think through problems on their own and come for discussion. They feel involved in the decision-making process. No one feels a loss of face in losing an argument because they treat these sessions as a learning experience.'

Acquiring new attitudes

I see no reason why Simple should take offence at my advice to expatriate managers to try to be mentors rather than masters. Also, no criticism is intended in my advice to families that they should try to assimilate into local communities. I had once offered this advice in the form of a letter in a column to a 7-year old called Caroline. She goes to a school meant mainly for expatriate children. Her mother, Australian by birth, has lived in Hong Kong all her life. Her father is Swiss and owns a small trading company. My letter ran as follows:

> I have been meaning to talk to you about a lot of things, but you are always so busy. There's school and piano or ballet lessons, then homework or a birthday party to go to. Though you don't like ballet classes, your mother wants you to grow up to be a lady. But if you would like to learn other things, too, never think you can't or shouldn't just because someone says they are only for boys. Women today are astronauts, engineers, doctors, pilots, and politicians. Don't limit your choices to what girls did in the past.
>   You remember the day when you were waiting after school for your father to pick you up? Another girl was standing alone. I think she was from Sri Lanka and one of the few Asian students in your school. Why don't you talk to her sometimes and find out more about her beautiful country? I am sure you also have some Chinese schoolmates. Hong Kong is their home, you know, and they will be here when your other

friends have gone. Don't forget that Hong Kong is your home, too. Even if you leave, you will always remember it. So why not make some good friends who will still be here in case you decide to come back for a visit?

I know you don't get a chance to make too many local friends. The club where you swim has few Asian children, and I think it is sad that your schoolbooks don't teach anything about Hong Kong or China or anywhere else in Asia. We'll all be proud if you become a great ballerina. But don't forget there are so many other things to do and learn. My hope is that you grow up to be not only a lady but a woman who knows enough about the wider world to help improve it.

In the form of my letter to Caroline I was obviously warning against spending life in expatriate ghettos. An Australian manager, David Brent, who used to be an advertising and market-research executive in Singapore and Malaysia had written to me on the same theme. He had grown up in Malaya and therefore understood its multiracial, multilingual society. He felt that he had an immense advantage as an Australian manager in being able to appreciate the customs, values, religions, and humour of the people. Newly arriving fellow-countrymen, he observed, made terrible mistakes, habitually trying to apply general principles to local problems. 'They deceived themselves by thinking they were making an effective and sustained contribution. But all too often in their closeted world contaminated by self-sufficient smugness they were lulled into a false sense of satisfaction.' What made things worse, Brent explained, was that Australian companies tried to manage their Asian operations from Sydney or Melbourne. They did not see that, while it may be practical to coordinate finance, expertise, and overall intelligence from head office, it was essential that local management serve customers and develop business. Effective control from Sydney would be no more possible than for a New York head office to run its Australian operations directly from New York. Brent illustrated his point with the story of a marketing failure in Australia in the early 1970s, when he was a strategist involved in the launch of an instant mashed potato. The locally proposed brand name, 'Potato Whip', was well received, while 'Smash', the name the London-based multinational was using elsewhere, had a very poor response. But head office forced it through and 'Smash' had to be withdrawn.

The head of the expatriate division of Shell UK, David Wheatley, makes the same point in a different way:

When I first joined the company 26 years ago, people going abroad automatically found themselves in the higher strata of society; the atmosphere was rather ex-colonial and they could more or less behave as they did back home. But as independence has spread throughout the

Third World countries, attitudes have had to alter. Shell no longer owns large operations overseas—it has to work in partnership with national ones.

Foreign companies serious about participating in the economic growth of Asia will have to become increasingly aware that competitiveness is not simply a function of who has the best technology, products, or pricing position. Internationally trained and culturally sensitive managers will be their greatest strength. But it will require a sustained effort and top management commitment on their part to develop these managers. The need may be easy to define but to translate it into a reality is often a most difficult task. Says Konrad Weis, president and chief executive officer, Bayer USA Inc. 'It takes perseverance and leadership from top management to communicate the view that internationalism is good, provincialism is bad.' Developing international managers is a long-term commitment, is expensive, and is sometimes a very sensitive issue, he adds.

It is fashionable these days to talk about 'paradigm shifts'. Organisations go into decline at the peak of their success because they fail to perceive and act on emerging patterns. As victims of 'paradigm paralysis', their thinking remains frozen in old patterns. Early identification of emerging paradigms is an essential component of improving the ability to anticipate. I believe a realisation that a new set of attributes is needed for an international manager to succeed in Asia today is the most important shift required in the thinking of large multinational corporations.

Speaking to the Beta Gamma Sigma National Honour Society, at the University of Hawaii, on the subject of the management needs of the pacific century, Dr James Walker, former president of Exxon Chemical Asia Pacific, urged the students to remember that Asia was no longer the continent that their parents or grandparents knew. Apart from social changes, the evolving patterns of economic development include a high number of joint ventures, increased local manufacture (both for export and import substitution), decreased dependence on raw material exports, and the establishment of a greater number of Asia-Pacific offices by multinationals. 'For years many American multinational companies have preferred the route of providing the three basics required to satisfy a specific foreign market—money, management, and technology—and to own the business 100 per cent, Walker said. 'Today we see very few 100 per cent foreign-owned ventures in Asia-Pacific. I am a strong believer that the best hope for success is for nationals to supply as much as possible of the three basics and the foreign partner to bring the part not available locally.' He stressed that the most important elements of successful participation are and will continue to be management resources and cultural sensitivity.

Learning to respect differences

Unfortunately, many multinationals continue to be overwhelmed by the myth of universality. Despite different lifestyles, they·maintain, all human beings are the same in that they need food, clothing, and shelter. But this is a simplistic statement. Everyday business problems and their solutions amply demonstrate that the reality is more complex and that people approach the same situation differently. In her book *For Richer, for Poorer*, Dr Ellen Frost introduces what she calls a mischievous metaphor: 'The characteristic American response to a world crisis is to jump up on the table and make a speech, while the characteristic Japanese response is to crawl under the table and quietly build a consensus.'

Western psychology has for long maintained that human nature is basically the same everywhere. But now there is growing awareness among psychotherapists that in focusing on similarities they have ignored crucial differences. In his book *In Search of Self in India and Japan*, Alan Roland, a New York psychoanalyst, states that many differences stem from the Western emphasis on raising children to be independent. This contrasts with the Asian focus on cultivating an intense emotional closeness. Asian children sleep with their mothers during the first four or five years. They are always in the company of a nurturing family member and are indulged in their whims. As they grow, they are 'scolded, shamed, physically punished, to make sure they fit themselves into the strict hierarchy of the culture'. Dr Roland adds that 'Compared to Americans, there's much less of a sense of an individual self among Asians. They experience themselves as far more embedded in a net of extremely close emotional relationships. They have what might be called a familial self.' Personal relationships tend to be both more subtle and more complex than the Westerners are used to. 'You expect others to sense what's going on in you without your having to say anything directly.' In contrast to the West, where people strive for inner consistency, in Asia people are more comfortable with selves that vary according to the particular relationship. 'This may be the biggest area of East-West misunderstanding,' warns Dr Roland.

Ken Sasaki, associate professor at Osaka City University, observes that it is by no means certain that the activities of the multinationals in Asia will truly help the region realise the great expectations for its steady economic growth:

> On close inspection, the proposition that multinationals can blend smoothly into different nations is intrinsically unsound. An organisational setup that consists of a large number of autonomous subsidiaries operating under a variety of forms of government and

management climates, employing many workers of different nationalities under completely disparate sets of labour-management practices—and that expects all these subsidiaries to act as one coordinated whole in line with the strategy and ideology of the corporate headquarters—carries from the outset the seeds of conflict with the subsidiaries' host countries.

Sasaki adds that as the subsidiaries grow in size, they could be seen as embodiments of the chauvinism and racism of the investor country. This has the potential to escalate the confrontations to a nation-to-nation level. Multinationals in Asia make use of the low wages, long working hours, and underdevelopment of modern democratic labour relations in the host countries. Says Sasaki:

> Their investment strategy operates on the premise that people in developing countries are less than fully aware of the problems of environmental destruction, pollution, and urbanisation that go hand in hand with industrialisation. The national awakening to these problems that is sure to occur in the near future will shake the foundations of the multinationals' activities.

But there are signs that multinationals are realising the significant changes that have taken place around us. Reuben Mark, CEO of Colgate-Palmolive, which derives 64 per cent of its revenues from outside the USA, says:

> Setting up in new countries is different from how it used to be. Once, you dropped an American off in Venezuela or Thailand with a boatload of toothpaste and had him build a business. Now we go into partnership with local business people or the local government. The fundamental difficulty is how to execute a global strategy and still allow those leading the local entity to feel they are controlling their own destiny.

Looking to the future, Mark adds in a *Fortune* magazine interview:

> The essence of business as we move into the twenty-first century is going to be tapping the talent of good people. It's not about where you locate the plants, it's how you locate the best people and motivate them. How do you trust them and have them trust you? It's certainly not easy, but communication and bridging cultural gaps is the top priority.

The CEO of Corning, James Houghton, warns that companies simply can't prosper in a diverse, multicultural world unless they reflect that diversity to some degree:

> As companies reflect more cultural diversity, they will become more tolerant, more willing to use differences, rather than sameness, as the

criteria for individual success within the organisation. Any business climate in which broadly different individuals may succeed will be a climate where the whole organisation prospers.

Becoming multicultural

Why don't more companies follow such sound advice? Ironically, it's due to a fear of change. Powerful multinationals who are radically changing the world in which we live are fearful of treating their Asian managers as equals. The fear arises from a fundamental lack of knowledge of culture, people, and institutions. The global syndrome of management calls for a uniform set of qualities in managers. As reflected on performance appraisal forms, these qualities are based on Western values. Peter Tan, a middle manager with a multinational in Singapore describes it as the 'Westernisation index'. He believes that to rise from the position of a marketing manager to a senior executive level, an Asian employee has had to adopt a completely Western style of behaviour. Asian middle managers have already demonstrated ability and intelligence to get where they are today. 'Why does their development stop at that level?' he asks.

Miyoshi Yo, president of H.B. Fuller Japan Co. Ltd., told me that the process stops because at a certain level the Asian managers begin to pose a challenge to the expatriate managers. Miyoshi once worked with the Japanese subsidiary of a French company. He quit because the French managers working with him in Tokyo zealously guarded their positions to the detriment of Miyoshi's prospects as promised by head office at the time he joined the company. 'When I went to Paris for my interview, top management told me that I spoke wonderful French and that French subsidiaries in Japan should be run by Japanese who understood both Japanese and European cultures,' says Miyoshi. 'So, I decided to leave Sumitomo which was a very big decision for me. At that time there were six French managers with the company in Japan. Two years later, there were nine. So I started wondering whether the promise made two years ago was real.' Miyoshi adds, 'The French managers did not like me very much because I was the only Japanese who spoke French. It was very disturbing to them because French was a tool for them to stick to their privileged positions in the Japanese organisation. Before me, no Japanese was able to communicate with Paris. They felt uneasy with me around.' Miyoshi stresses that the Japanese managers are not treated equally. 'Where there are many foreign managers, they tend to protect their privileged positions.'

A Hong Kong manager, Bill Yuen, who works with one of the largest international accounting firms, reiterates this point: 'Most foreign companies paint a rosy picture of future prospects. They always say there will be ample opportunities for everyone as the business grows. But when the business grows, they bring in more expatriates.' Yuen firmly believes that the brain drain is not entirely due to 1997. 'Sometimes, management says we are too preoccupied with the present and fail to see future prospects. Well, I am 45 years old and my desire to become a partner in the firm has nothing to do with 1997. I believe I am at the peak of my professional ability and can be most helpful to my company as a local partner.'

Multinational organisations are a great phenomena of our times. They are providing the engine for world economic growth. Their subsidiaries throughout the world are successful in almost everything —technology, manufacturing, marketing, and distribution—except human relations. It is wrong to call a company multinational just because it has manufacturing or marketing operations in several countries. If the United Nations, for instance, had only a couple of members but had offices in 50 countries, one would not call it the United Nations. The United States Information Service has offices in most countries, but one can't call it a multinational information service. A true multinational company must be one which has absorbed several cultures. Only those organisations which are able to become multicultural will survive and prosper in the pacific century.

Index